THE LITTLE BOOK OF
CONSPIRACIES

THE LITTLE BOOK OF
CONSPIRACIES

50 OF THE WORLD'S GREATEST THEORIES

JOEL LEVY

METRO BOOKS
NEW YORK

METRO BOOKS
New York

An Imprint of Sterling Publishing
387 Park Avenue South
New York, NY 10016

METRO BOOKS and the distinctive Metro Books logo are trademarks of Sterling Publishing Co., Inc

© 2005 by Elwin Street Limited

Conceived and produced by
Elwin Street Limited
144 Liverpool Road
London N1 1LA
www.elwinstreet.com

This 2008 edition published by Metro Books by arrangement with Elwin Street Limited.

Design and icon illustration: Jon Wainwright
All other illustrations: Richard Burgess

Picture credits Getty Images: pages 20, 62, 64, 66, 68; HAARP
(www.haarp.alaska.edu): page 133; NASA: page 117 (top); Science
Photo Library: pages 13, 120

ISBN 978-1-4351-0652-9

For information about custom editions, special sales, and premium and corporate purchases, please
contact Sterling Special Sales at 800-805-5489 or specialsales@sterlingpublishing.com.

Manufactured in China

4 6 8 10 9 7 5 3

www.sterlingpublishing.com

Contents

Introduction

*"In politics, nothing happens by accident.
If it happened, you can bet it was
planned that way."*

Franklin Delano Roosevelt, 32nd US President

In this honest look at parapolitics—to give "conspiracy theories" a name that is a shade more respectable—author Joel Levy compresses the labyrinthine arguments surrounding the most compelling theories from around the world. The field-guide format allows immediate access to the essential facts currently being debated by theorists and debunkers everywhere. Instead of spectacle, Levy delivers data. The discussion is accessible to those who simply want to understand more about what's behind the headlines. Conspiracies that are often distorted in many sensationalized ways, Levy pares down with concise analysis and reaching commonsense conclusions. He does not embrace every theory as absolute truth but neither does he dismiss them as total bunk.

Consider only a few of the subjects: the development of auto-immune disease as a weapon of biowarfare or a population-specific manipulation by the pharmaceutical industry; that government officials either planned the flying of jetliners into skyscrapers on 9/11 or allowed it to happen with stand-down orders; the multi-tiered, transnational loyalties of possibly mind-controlled political assassins. Readers might encounter such things also in the plot summaries found in the booklets of an *X-Files* DVD, but they resemble more the demons that drive the plots of *Buffy the Vampire Slayer* than the reality of these phenomena. The process of transforming important parapolitical topics into light-hearted spectacle comes as part of the overall conspiracy of the media conglomerates to trivialize them—as any good conspiracy theorists would point out. Hence the need for this pocket guide.

Even though the complexity of conspiracy as a topic has resisted being compressed into such a small tome until now, the growth of conspiracy as an entertainment genre certainly has produced enough fodder to call for a return of the pocket format. *The Little Book of Conspiracies* offers a refreshingly nuanced approach to a popular and compelling field whose followers are legion and whose fascination never wanes.

Kenn Thomas, editor, *Steamshovel* magazine

Part One:

It Could Be
Happening To You

The Fluoride Con

Corporate America is getting away with massive industrial pollution by forcing people to drink fluoride for their "health."

Since the 1950s, many authorities in the United States, and others around the world, have added fluoride to water supplies in a large-scale public-health drive to reduce tooth decay levels. The American Dental Association, the World Health Organization, the British government, and many other bodies insist that fluoridating drinking water reduces tooth decay and does not cause health problems.

What the theorists say

The evidence supporting fluoridation is severely flawed. Although some research is now dated, and more recent studies generally favor fluoridation, there are findings that call the validity of such research into question and suggest that children, for example, are consuming too much fluoride. Skeptics point to claims that scientists who speak out against the pro-fluoride establishment are bullied or pressured into changing their findings.

Even at relatively low concentrations, fluoride has been linked to bone-density loss, cancer, poisoning, and dental problems. Toxic lead concentrations in drinking water have been traced back to the presence of fluoride, which strips the protective coating inside lead pipes. Since most of the fluoride added to public water supplies is produced as a byproduct of industries such as aluminum and steel processing and fertilizer manufacture, it is a pollutant laden with toxic substances such as arsenic, lead, and other heavy metals.

If fluoridation has questionable health benefits—and may actually be toxic—why is the establishment keen for us to believe otherwise? Because of big business. Since the 1930s, industrial giants such as US Steel and the Aluminum Company of America (ALCOA) started to run into trouble with accusations of damaging pollution leading to ruinous lawsuits. Fluoride was a "problem" pollutant, linked to everything from contaminated farmland to wholesale health calamities, such as the notorious 1948 Donora Death Fog— a pall of polluted air that killed 20 and poisoned thousands of residents in Donora, Pennsylvania, home of the massive US steel and zinc works. Handling their fluoride byproducts properly and cleaning up contaminated areas would cost the US industry billions of dollars, while admitting the potential health implications would open them to crippling union actions.

The sly solution was to market fluoride as a public health benefit. At the time, there was a lot of interest in findings which showed that residents of areas with high levels of natural water fluoridation seemed to suffer less from tooth decay, leading to the first suggestions that artificial fluoridation might be beneficial. The US Public Health Service was in favor of this proposal, but who was in charge of the FSA? None other than Oscar R. Ewing, former top lawyer for ALCOA. Other senior figures in the push to promote the dental benefits of fluoride also had links to ALCOA.

The official line

Pro-fluoridation voices argue that studies, old and new, do not prove it is a health threat, and that there is plenty of evidence to show a marked improvement in dental wellbeing across two generations; also that anti-fluoridation research tends to be characterized by poor science.

How paranoid should you be? 31%

According to Dr. Robert Carton of the US Environmental Protection Agency, "Fluoridation is the greatest case of scientific fraud of this century, if not of all time." With claims such as these, it is hard not to see the establishment's reluctance to question the fluoride orthodoxy as, at best, a severe case of inertia—an unwillingness to admit error. To believe the more lurid claims that the establishment is colluding with big business in marketing poisonous pollution as medicine to avoid a large-scale clean-up, you would have to be convinced the elite would put profit before public interest. In an era of Enron, who could believe such a thing?

Sweet Poison

Web-based activists claim that
aspartame, the artificial sweetener
more commonly known as NutraSweet,
is extremely toxic.

The artificial sweetener aspartylphenylalanine-methyl-ester (aka aspartame) was accidentally created by chemists working for pharmaceuticals giant GD Searle in 1965. Hundreds of times sweeter than sugar, aspartame is now used in almost 5,000 products around the world and is best known as NutraSweet.

What the theorists say

Aspartame is an excitotoxin, a substance that stimulates nerve cells. It also breaks down in the body to produce methanol, which is converted into formaldehyde, an extremely potent poison that can cause a range of symptoms from headaches and tremors to acute vision impairment and blindness as well as diabetes. This "aspartame disease" is often misdiagnosed as systemic lupus or multiple sclerosis. Aspartame has also been linked to cancer and brain damage.

Despite all this, the US Food and Drug Administration (FDA) approved the use of aspartame in the 1970s, and all the other regulatory bodies of the world have followed suit. Supposedly this happened because GD Searle falsified or concealed unfavorable research into the substance and also used political muscle to get approval. In charge of GD Searle at the time was none other than Donald Rumsfeld. Other companies that now make millions from aspartame include such corporate "villains" as Ajinomoto (manufacturer of monosodium glutamate) and Monsanto. Suspiciously, a former head of the FDA now has a senior post at Monsanto. Collectively, this corrupt nexus of big business and politics conspires to suppress the truth about aspartame.

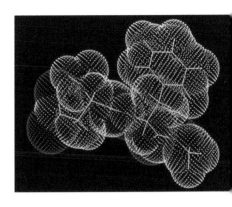

Right Model of a molecule of aspartame, which is widely used as a sweetener in drinks.

The official line

The anti-aspartame campaign is characterized by poor or nonsense science, misrepresentation, and unsupported anecdote. The substance is composed of two harmless amino acids and breaks down in the digestive system to produce these components, together with a minuscule and biologically insignificant quantity of methanol. As a general guideline, the methanol produced by drinking a can of sweetened soda is half that contained in a glass of tomato juice. You would have to drink at least 240 liters at one time to consume a dangerous amount. As for the other claims, numerous studies by every conceivable regulatory body and health watchdog from the *Lancet* to the Multiple Sclerosis Society dismiss them and aspartame has been repeatedly deemed safe by the FDA, the United Nations, the World Health Organization, and the European Union. Numerous well-conducted studies have shown no ill effects from aspartame, even at high concentrations, with repeated doses, or even with subjects who previously claimed aspartame was making them ill.

How paranoid should you be? 9%

The weight of opinion from informed, disinterested sources comes down in favor of aspartame, although paranoiacs claim the FDA is corrupt and that other regulatory bodies have followed suit, ignoring any "negative" findings. They even claim that organizations such as the Multiple Sclerosis Society and diabetes support groups have a vested interest in propagating the conditions caused by aspartame. While there are probably still many unanswered questions about the relationship between big pharmaceuticals and the US government, aspartame is almost certainly a safe substance for all but a handful of extremely susceptible individuals.

The Truth About AIDS

Groups as diverse as the KGB, white supremacists, and the Nation of Islam have claimed HIV/AIDS to be a manmade epidemic. Can they possibly be right?

After the Acquired Immune Deficiency Syndrome (AIDS) epidemic began in the early 1980s, a consensus arose claiming it was caused by the Human Immunodeficiency Virus (HIV), an infection that had probably originated in African green monkeys and jumped the genetic barrier to humans either through contact or direct consumption of "bushmeat." When AIDS arrived in the West, it spread within certain sections of society—among homosexuals, drug users, and the black community.

What the theorists say

The pattern in which AIDS has affected specific communities within our population has led different groups to propose the theory that HIV was created by someone with a vendetta against homosexuals, blacks, and/or drug users. According to the anti-Semitic Nation of Islam, HIV was engineered by the Jews as a tool for visiting genocide on blacks.

According to KGB disinformation disseminated in the 1980s and subsequently picked up by many Western conspiracy theorists, HIV was "manufactured" at US chemical and biological warfare laboratories and used by the CIA to target "undesirable" sections of the population.

South African President Thabo Mbeki declared in the late 1990s that AIDS was not provoked by HIV at all but was a disease caused by poverty and the experimental medicines of white-owned pharmaceutical companies. Some more credible authorities, such as Robert Gallo, the scientist who first isolated HIV, have suggested links to vaccination programs, such as the experimental anti-hepatitis B vaccination program tested on American gay men in the late 1970s, or the massive 1966 to 1977 World Health

Organization (WHO) African anti-smallpox vaccination program. Believers in the latter scenario cast the WHO as an agent of the Illuminati (see pages 77–78) using the United Nations as a front for a new world order.

If the very idea of a group such as the US government deliberately inflicting a deadly plague on its own citizens sounds far-fetched, remember that it did just this in the Tuskegee experiment, a 40-year-long study that began in the 1930s, where poor Southern blacks with syphilis were monitored but left untreated and uninformed about their condition, allowing them to transmit the disease to their wives and children so doctors could study the effects.

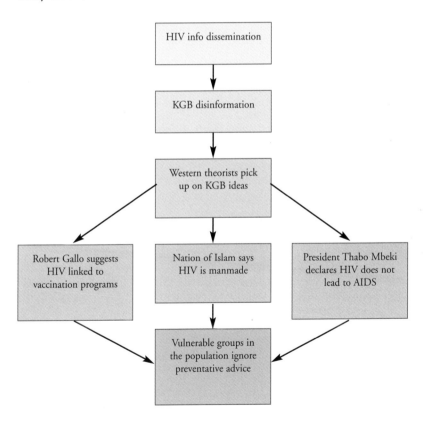

The official line

The mainstream medical establishment points out the countless scientific, historical, and epidemiological holes in such conspiracy arguments. Many of the theorists claim HIV was engineered by combining a sheep and a human retrovirus. HIV, however, bears no resemblance to the former but does share a close family similarity to known monkey retroviruses.

Conspiracy theorists argue that AIDS appeared so suddenly in the 1980s that it cannot have been a naturally spreading pandemic and they also query how it came to the US from Africa. In fact, AIDS cases dating back to the 1950s have now been identified and the relevant medical literature suggests cases dating back even further. Several of the early AIDS victims seem to have been sailors, suggesting an obvious transmission route to the gay and drug-using communities. Although HIV/AIDS had its biggest initial impact on homosexuals, drug users, and blacks, this was only a reflection of the more severe health and drug-abuse problems suffered by these communities for social and economic reasons.

How paranoid should you be? 0%

The HIV/AIDS conspiracy theory holds little water but it has had a devastating impact on prevention efforts among some of the highest-risk groups. People who work with black prisoners, for instance, have reported that an alarming number ignore preventative advice because of the conspiracy theories they have heard. These observations are sobering examples of how the rhetoric of conspiracy and paranoia can be employed to further the ideology and agendas of extremist groups with incredibly harmful consequences. Who knows how many millions of people in Africa, America, and around the world are needlessly infected with HIV because they believed the conspiracy theories and ignored the preventative advice that could have saved them?

Total Information Awareness

Every action by American citizens is constantly being monitored through advanced technology by an Orwellian government.

In the wake of 9/11, the US Department of Defense set up a new program called the Office of Information Awareness (OIA) headed by Admiral John Poindexter. Its stated aim was to develop and implement Total Information Awareness (TIA), a project that would use the most advanced technology to collect, analyze, and store as much information as possible about everyone. Funding for the project was eventually dropped in response to opposition from the Democrats and American civil liberties groups.

What the theorists say

Everything about the OIA and its TIA program confirmed the worst Orwellian nightmares of those who viewed the US government with suspicion. The original logo of the OIA (see page 18) was the Masonic all-seeing eye pyramid from the Great Seal, casting its gaze over the globe and emblazoned with the motto *scientia est potentia*, "knowledge is power." It was quietly dropped and replaced, and the name of the project was changed to Terrorist Information Awareness (hardly reassuring).

The role of Poindexter rang alarm bells—he was the highest-ranking official to be convicted of involvement in the Iran-Contra scandal and was also highly placed in an IT company that stood to win a lucrative business contract from the OIA.

The awesome scope of the TIA project meant that every individual in America could expect to have every detail of his or her life recorded and picked over by intelligence analysts. Related programs included new technology to identify people at a distance from their gait or appearance, and systems that could transcribe and translate speech in any language.

Poindexter has since resigned and apparently the OIA has been wrapped up. Many of the TIA's subprograms, however, continue to be funded and who knows what sort of covert activities continue beyond Congressional oversight?

The official line
In the post-9/11 world, imaginative new approaches for tackling terrorism and preserving security are essential. The aims of the TIA were only ever counterterrorist and there would have been safeguards to protect privacy and civil liberties. Since the program was shelved, and the OIA no longer exists, it is no longer an issue.

How paranoid should you be? 92%
No ban was imposed on developing TIA for use against non-American activity and development has continued on similar projects for use against US citizens. Perhaps most alarming is the fact that a form of the program has existed for more than 50 years. The National Security Agency's Echelon project is a top-secret telecommunications monitoring system that has been around since 1947. The US, in partnership with the UK, Australia, New Zealand, and Canada, operates a global network of spy stations that tap into all forms of electronic communication. The next time that you are refused entry to the US for no apparent reason, try to recall whether you once made disparaging remarks about the President in a phone call, or glanced at a website critical of US policy. Chances are "they" know all about it.

Right The original logo for OIA, the Masonic all-seeing eye pyramid from the Great Seal. This logo was quickly replaced.

Anthrax A-Go-Go

Murky rumors surround the US anthrax scare. How much did the government know? And why did White House staff take anti-anthrax medication on 9/11?

In late 2001, following the 9/11 terrorist attacks, a number of anthrax-filled letters were mailed to key media and political targets in the US. Five people eventually died and 17 others were infected. The perpetrators were never caught and the source of the attacks remains a mystery.

What the theorists say

In the absence of any actual explanation, accusations and suspicions have filled the vacuum. Paranoid suspicions were inflamed by an agency report claiming some White House staff were given Cipro, the anti-anthrax antibiotic, on September 11. No explanation has been forthcoming and the Bush Administration has obstructed any attempts under the Freedom of Information Act to find out more. A number of leads suggest a link between the mailings and Al-Qaeda or Saddam Hussein. The Iraq connection was first suggested by Larry Wayne Harris, a man with far-right links arrested in 1998 for possession of anthrax. He claimed that a prominent Iraqi had warned him that Saddam was using Iraqi women to smuggle anthrax into the US in order to attack the government. Several Iraqis were supposedly arrested and tested positive.

Most theorists, however, regard these observations as smokescreens because the real culprits were American far-right extremists, possibly in cahoots with government insiders. The strain of anthrax used in the attacks was identified as coming from the US military's own stocks, although the CIA have vehemently denied this. The targets of the mailings were liberal politicians or the media (vilified by far-right extremists). Far-right groups are known to have made efforts to get hold of anthrax stocks via Harris.

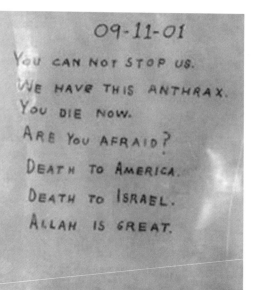

09-11-01
You CAN NOT STOP US.
WE HAVE THIS ANTHRAX.
You DIE NOW.
ARE YOU AFRAID?
DEATH TO AMERICA.
DEATH TO ISRAEL.
ALLAH IS GREAT.

Left A letter sent to Senate Majority Leader Tom Daschle in October 2001, which contained anthrax.

Adding to the stew are allegations that vaccine manufacturers with government links have attempted to profit from the climate of fear after the attacks. How did the mailers effectively get their hands on such high-grade, professionally prepared anthrax and why has no one been caught?

The official line

"They" say remarkably little, supposedly because not much more is known about exactly what happened and how. There is official confusion over the likely source of the anthrax and the mailings. The investigation is presumably ongoing.

How paranoid should you be? 82%

The Bush Administration was happy to let circulate rumors connecting the anthrax mailings to Al-Qaeda and/or Saddam, knowing it would strengthen public support for their plans in the Middle East. On the other hand, allowing public focus to shift to domestic right-wing extremists did not fit their agenda, and perhaps this explains the lack of success of the official investigation. Then there is still that mystery of White House staffers taking Cipro on 9/11.

Nigerian Polio Vaccine Controversy

A health drive or sinister plot to depopulate Africa? Nigerian Muslims raised questions about the true purpose of a UN vaccination program.

The predominantly Muslim state of Kano in northern Nigeria is the epicenter of the world's biggest and fastest-growing polio epidemic, radiating out from northern Nigeria to at least seven west and central African states. In late 2003, a massive new push by the World Health Organization (WHO), funded chiefly by the US government, to distribute doses of polio vaccine to 60 million children, centered on Kano, where the number of cases had increased by an alarming 30 percent on the previous year. The Nigerian vaccination drive was crucial to the WHO's goal of eradicating polio worldwide by the end of 2004.

What the theorists say

Kano is led by an extreme Islamist governor and ruled under Islam's sharia law, a theocracy autonomous from the rest of Nigeria. There is a strong tradition of mistrust toward the US (as there is throughout the Islamic world), and in December 2003, this malaise manifested itself in an unexpected and alarming fashion.

Muslim clerics in the region circulated warnings that the polio vaccines offered by the WHO were contaminated in some way, or were not even vaccines but toxic chemicals, and that the vaccination program was a front for a US-inspired WHO plot to make Muslim women in Kano infertile. According to Datti Ahmed, President of the Sharia Supreme Council in Kano, "The vaccine is part of a US-led conspiracy to depopulate the developing world."

The state government, led by governor Ibrahim Shekarau, declined to take part in the program. When a panel convened by the Nigerian government insisted that the claims were unfounded and the vaccine safe, Kano state government spokesperson Sule Yau Sule was skeptical, telling reporters, "With due respect, I believe our professionals know better."

Not until July 2004, once local "experts" had tested a batch of vaccine prepared in the Muslim country Indonesia and proclaimed it to be safe, did Kano relent and allow the vaccination program to continue on the basis that only Indonesian vaccine would be used.

The official line

The WHO indignantly denied being part of a US-hatched plot and insisted their vaccines were safe, as did the Nigerian government, backed by a panel of experts convened to test the vaccines. UNICEF spokespeople discussed the dangers the embargo visited upon both Nigerians and the citizens of surrounding states. Sadly, their concerns were well-founded, and by the time the Kano authorities relented and the program got under way, Nigeria had three-quarters of the world's polio cases and the disease was being transmitted at the fastest rate ever recorded.

How paranoid should you be? 0%

To many in the West, the Kano Muslim claims about the vaccination drive seem absurd and several commentators have criticized the state's leadership for playing politics with people's lives. The episode is partly the result of local tensions, but it is also indicative of the level of belief in conspiracy theories present throughout the Muslim world. Like the widespread belief in HIV/AIDS conspiracy theories (see pages 14–15), the real victims of this triumph of suspicion over science are always the most vulnerable in our society.

Is the CIA Peddling Drugs?

The CIA orchestrates the production, traffic, and sales of drugs, in order to obtain covert funding and oppress ethnic minorities in the US.

Persistent rumors about the CIA's role in illegal drug traffic in various parts of the world came to a head with the accusations about the Iran-Contra affair that surfaced in a series of articles in the *San Jose Mercury News* in 1996. These alleged that CIA operatives had trafficked thousands of kilos of cocaine into California for conversion into crack and then used the proceeds to fund the Nicaraguan Contra insurrection.

What the theorists say

The CIA's involvement in drug trafficking began with its wartime alliance with the Mafia and continued when CIA-trained Chinese paramilitaries failed to invade China and took up residence in the Burmese jungle where they started growing opium and producing heroin. During the Vietnam War, other CIA-funded paramilitaries started doing the same thing in countries like Thailand and Laos. Conspiracy theorists claim, for example, the CIA used "Air America," its undercover airline dedicated to ship supplies to anti-Communist allies in the region, to help ferry drugs to various shipping points.

Florida-based, CIA-linked Mafiosi were brought in to traffic the drugs to America. The CIA used the massive profits as covert funding and the drugs were dumped into ethnic minority communities to help keep them quiescent and downtrodden.

The pattern was repeated in the late 1970s and 1980s in Central America. When Socialist rebels finally kicked the long-established, US-backed Somoza regime from Nicaragua, the CIA formed a paramilitary force called the Contras to wage a brutal terrorist insurgency.

When Congress specifically outlawed US funding for these Nicaraguan mercenaries, the CIA needed to find another way of paying for the whole operation. This paved the way for Contra drug smugglers to carry cocaine into the US on flights arranged by the CIA to help guarantee a smooth passage of goods. To open up a new market for cocaine (at that point a low-volume, high-cost narcotic), the CIA groomed drug dealers in crack cocaine production and hooked them up with street gangs.

The official line

The 1996 newspaper allegations stung the Agency into launching a wide-ranging investigation that found none of the named principals to have links with the CIA or to know anything about the Contras' drug-trafficking operations. Perhaps some junior field operatives knew about one or two shady characters on the Contra side, but in the interest of fighting Communism, they had to turn a blind eye.

How paranoid should you be? 75%

Even if the CIA never intended to support drug trafficking in any of its operation zones, it still begs this question: What happens when you train up a group of criminals into an organized militia, arm them to the teeth, and then drop them in the middle of a lawless wilderness with an ecology ideal for growing drug crops (and with a long tradition of doing so), only to then tell them to figure out a way to fund themselves in the long term? Americans would call this a "no-brainer," yet it seems strange that the CIA made exactly the same mistake three times (counting Afghanistan, see pages 48–49), in the process creating the world's three main drug production centers.

Ultimately, the CIA was able to secure a new remit and massive extra funding to fight a "war" on the very drug operations they had initiated. The administrator of the DEA, federal judge Robert Banner, actually said in an interview, "What the CIA did is drug smuggling. It's illegal."

Detroit vs the Electric Car

Car manufacturers and oil producers collude to suppress the development of environmentally friendly alternatives to the internal-combustion engine.

In the late nineteenth and early twentieth century, electric cars predated and outperformed petrol-driven vehicles. The arrival of the internal-combustion engine then made a small cartel of manufacturing and oil-producing giants extremely rich. Ever since, increasing concerns about vanishing fossil fuel stocks, unstable supply, environmental impact, and adverse health effects from pollution have led to pleas from outside the motor/oil industry for new forms of energy production and car propulsion to be developed and produced. Even today, however, true electric cars remain a minority product.

What the theorists say

The motor and oil industry have a vested interest in maintaining our reliance on expensive combustion-engine-based technology, irrespective of its impact on our wallets, health, or environment. Over the last century, these industries have suppressed mainstream research into alternative energy sources that might provide cheap, clean energy available to everyone with minimal infrastructure. Nonetheless, numerous independent researchers and inventors have stumbled upon viable technologies, only to have their work bought out and/or destroyed by the corporate behemoths. If the inventors refuse to sell, their research is denigrated, they are ridiculed and, as a last resort, they may even be murdered.

The major motor manufacturers also colluded to obstruct governmental moves that would challenge the status quo. The best-attested example was during the Great Smog Conspiracy of the 1950s and 1960s. Smog, primarily caused by exhaust fumes, was a steadily worsening problem in California and local-government health officials there and elsewhere put pressure on Detroit to improve emissions standards. The big car manufacturers announced a joint effort to overcome the problem, but in private agreed not to force each other's hands and to effectively discourage emission-control research. Behind the scenes, they lobbied fiercely to head off federal legislation requiring them to make changes. The motivation for all this was quite simple really: they feared it would cost too much money and eat into their profits.

But how does the Smog Conspiracy come to bear on the electric car debate? In 1991, three big Detroit car manufacturers got together and formed the Advanced Battery Consortium, a joint initiative to help develop electric cars, which was deeply reminiscent of the joint smog initiative of the 1950s. Several commentators who saw the link pointed to the half-hearted and contradictory efforts made by the big motor companies to develop electric cars in the intervening years. Are things likely to change?

The official line

As far as "free energy" devices go, there is no such product. Claims to the contrary are pseudoscience, peddled by con men looking to swindle potential backers. As far as the electric car goes, there is no conspiracy, only market forces at work. Until battery technology makes radical advances, electric cars will not offer viable performance or cost alternatives to conventional power sources. Another consideration is the cost of the infrastructure that would allow routine battery charging. There are similar obstacles to other petrol-free technologies, such as fuel cells or hydrogen-powered cars. Where electrical technology can make an impact is in the new generation of hybrid vehicles. These are now competitive in price and performance and car manufacturers are promoting them enthusiastically, giving the lie to claims that they want to suppress new technology.

How paranoid should you be? 22%

The bitter experience of many fleeced investors, over hundreds of years, attests to the unreliability of free-energy claims. As for the anti-electric car conspiracy, it would have to be a global, multi-generational conspiracy that would overwhelmingly benefit OPEC countries. It is probably true, however, that manufacturing giants will resist potentially expensive changes until their hand is forced by either consumers or new legislation.

> The Ford engineering staff, although mindful that automobile engines produce gases, feels that these waste vapors are dissipated in the atmosphere quickly and do not present an air pollution problem ...
>
> FORD MOTOR CO. LETTER TO KENNETH HAHN, 1953

> ... The automobile manufacturers, through AMA, conspired not to compete in the research, development, manufacture, and installation of pollution control devices, and collectively did all in their power to delay such research, development, manufacturing, and installation.
>
> US DEPARTMENT OF JUSTICE CONFIDENTIAL MEMO, 1968

No Cure for Cancer?

A cure for cancer has been known for decades but there is a giant conspiracy by pharmaceutical companies to suppress this information.

More than 10 million people are diagnosed with cancer every year and the rate of incidence is continuously increasing; by 2020, it will reach 15 million a year. Cancer causes 12 percent of the world's deaths, a staggering 6 million every year. While treatment has improved dramatically over the last century, very few cases can actually be cured.

What the theorists say

The true causes of cancer and an easy cure have already been discovered.

According to one popular alternative health movement, medical pioneer Royal Raymond Rife (1888–1971) discovered back in the 1930s that cancer was caused by viruses and that these could be destroyed by using radionics, the science of electromagnetic vibrations in living organisms. As a result, the patient was completely cured, often just with a single treatment. When these methods started becoming too popular, the American Medical Association (AMA) and the American government launched a crusade against Rife, labeling him a quack and threatening the licences of doctors who used his machines.

An alternative view suggests that cancer is caused by a vitamin B16 (aka laetrile) deficiency, most commonly found in fruit pips, such as in apricots, and that in parts of the world where this type of fruit is a staple of the local diet, such as in parts of Central Asia, cancer is unknown. This information has been suppressed in the US, where pro-laetrile writings have been destroyed and court cases brought against laetrile supporters.

At the root of the cancer conspiracy are the vested interests of those groups who stand to gain most from perpetuating the scourge of cancer:

namely the pharmaceutical giants making huge profits from toxic, destructive anti-cancer drugs, who would not be able to patent alternative and/or natural treatments; cancer specialists, nurses, and hospitals, who would be out of a job if it could be cured; health insurance companies, whose services would be made redundant; and the government, which could even be using cancer as a population-control tool.

The official line

The cancer conspiracy theory falls down on two main counts: firstly, in terms of the science involved; secondly, with regard to the motivation and logistics of the supposed conspiracy.

None of the proposed cures for cancer stands up to any degree of scrutiny, and while they may be supported by anecdotal evidence, they have all failed

proper scientific tests. Rife's radionic approach is a good example. The scientist was simply developing the pattern of Dr. Albert Abrams, one of the greatest con men in medical history. Radionics is a classic pseudoscience: it uses convincing-sounding terms and plausible equipment and apparently passes rigorous tests, but only those tests designed and performed by

Left Royal Raymond Rife's Universal Microscope, which he presented to the world in 1933. He claimed that with it, and his groundbreaking development of radionics, he could cure cancer.

its proponents (for example, Rife's cancer-causing viruses could only be seen with his own specially devised apparatus—see page 29). One of the frequently repeated claims regarding these alternative therapies is that they are suppressed because they are able to offer cures that are virtually free. So why did Rife and his modern-day proponents charge so much money for their treatments and so jealously guard the secrets of radionic technology?

On a more general level, it is absurd and offensive to allege that the entire health and medical profession wishes to suppress possible cancer cures. Pharmaceutical companies are always on the lookout for new product development as the patents on their old drugs lapse, and if a natural cure is discovered, they will seek to isolate the active ingredient and try to improve on it. At least some doctors and nurses surely have positive motivations, and they could easily retrain for other branches of medicine if a cancer cure was found.

How paranoid should you be? 0%
It is better to be skeptical and suspicious about claims made by alternative health con artists looking to profit from the desperation of terminally ill patients. True, scientific orthodoxy is often resistant to change and slow to assimilate new advances, but this is a good thing and protects us from frauds and false avenues.

Chemtrails

The government and the military have been spraying mysterious substances into the atmosphere under cover of normal aircraft contrails.

Jet exhausts contain water vapor that condenses and freezes into tiny ice crystals at the low temperatures found at high altitudes, leaving a trail of condensation (a contrail) in a plane's wake. Normally contrails evaporate quickly, but in the past 20 years there has been increasing concern about "chemtrails" (lingering contrails), which spread slowly across the sky as if forming clouds. They are suspected to be a direct result of chemical spraying.

What the theorists say

The persistence and spread of these chemical trails cannot simply be explained away by atmospherical physics. They must be the result of something added to normal jet fuel or released separately as a form of high-altitude spray. People who live under such chemtrails report a range of illnesses, including chronic fatigue, cancer, and Alzheimer's. The trails are also associated with weird weather and strange falling filaments (sometimes called "angel hair"), gel, or soapy substances. The analysis of chemtrail fallout has supposedly revealed heavy metals, bacteria, and even red blood cells. Anyone around the world who takes the time to look up can see groups of aircraft laying down chemical trail "grids" to blanket urban areas.

Theories about why and who vary. Possibly the American government is trying to poison the general population, or maybe it is attempting some sort of mass vaccination. Alternatively, chemtrails are a form of weather control (cloud-seeding) or a measure for counteracting the effects of global warming. This is not mere science fiction. During the Cold War, both sides invested heavily in cloud-seeding technology, which today has reached high levels of sophistication. Documents in public records attest to the military's desire to

The Effects of Chemtrails

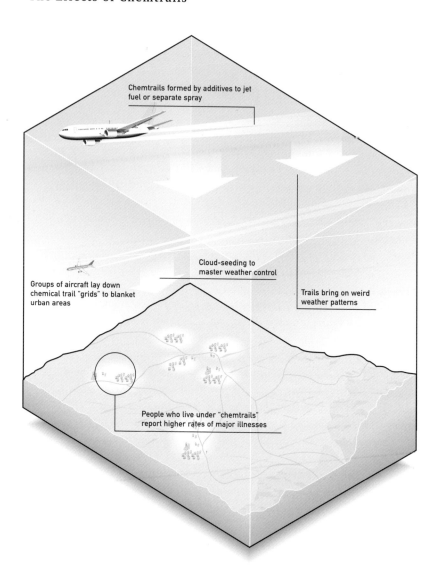

Chemtrails formed by additives to jet fuel or separate spray

Cloud-seeding to master weather control

Groups of aircraft lay down chemical trail "grids" to blanket urban areas

Trails bring on weird weather patterns

People who live under "chemtrails" report higher rates of major illnesses master weather-control, and in 1997, leading physicist Edward Teller, father of the H-bomb, publicized a plan to form high-altitude cloudscreens that could reflect heat back into space and help to reduce global warming.

In another explanation, supposed US Air Force insiders have revealed that chemtrails are laid out to produce conductive channels stretching for hundreds of miles that provide conduits for radio wave transmission and are possibly connected to the HAARP Aurora project (see pages 133–134).

The official line
If the atmosphere has a high water content, then a contrail will not vaporize. The ice crystals, together with soot particles in the exhaust, will act as seeds for more and bigger droplets, creating a long-lasting cloud that slowly spreads outward. Contrails are believed to be more prevalent now because of increased air traffic and possibly because the atmosphere is more humid.

"Angel hair" is a well-known natural phenomenon caused by baby spiders that hatch by the million and use strands of silk as parasails to achieve wind-borne dispersion. Contrail "grids" over cities are caused by heavy air traffic. Reports about chemtrail fallout and its supposed contents are not supported by the evidence. The radio-wave conduit explanation ignores the fact that existing technology, including satellites, makes this application pointless.

How paranoid should you be? 0%
Cloud-seeding technology probably does exist and it is likely that the military does carry out the testing of such technology. We also know that the US Air Force dropped "angel hair" strands to short-out power lines during the NATO bombing of Serbia, a hitherto classified technology. None of this is the same as saying that the world's governments, militaries, airlines, air authorities, and private aircraft owners are engaged in a huge conspiracy to experiment with this technology on a daily basis. It would be impossible to keep such a conspiracy secret. The simple truth is that 99 percent of chemtrails can be perfectly adequately explained by ordinary physics, and that while they may well be affecting the environment (ironically, by temporarily counteracting global warming, as per Teller's plan), they are not sinister.

Part Two:

Political Conspiracies and Colossal Cover-ups

Operation Stay Behind

A shady alliance of ex-Nazis and anti-communists sought to subvert post-war European politics through intimidation, intrigue, and violence.

Even before World War II was over, many on the US side were already viewing the Russians as enemies and planning for the next war—this time against Communism.

What the theorists say

The Americans recruited much of the former Nazi intelligence apparatus and personnel and set them up as the Gehlen Organization, led by former Nazi general Reinhard Gehlen, to form an anti-communist intelligence agency for West Germany. Gehlen used almost exclusively SS, Gestapo, and SD personnel, including some of the Nazi's worst war criminals. Meanwhile, around the rest of Europe, the Americans set up Operation Stay Behind, using a network of fascists (who were allowed to escape justice) to put in place an anti-communist infrastructure, which included spies, soldiers, and arms caches. Stay Behind cadres were operative in France, Belgium, and the Netherlands, but most actively in Italy, where the operation was named Gladio (from the Italian for "sword").

The rationale behind the movement was that, should the Soviets advance, the Stay Behind network would form the basis of the resistance, but this neo-fascist network soon showed its real colors, meddling in politics to combat the socialist and communist parties that were gaining ground through democratic means.

In France, for instance, they compiled blacklists of leftists and participated in attempts to assassinate the insufficiently anti-commie de Gaulle. In Italy the socialists gained more and more ground with the ballot box, so Operation Gladio resorted to a more and more violent "strategy of

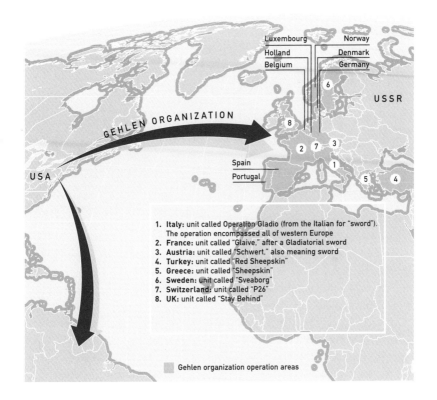

1. **Italy:** unit called Operation Gladio (from the Italian for "sword"). The operation encompassed all of western Europe
2. **France:** unit called "Glaive," after a Gladiatorial sword
3. **Austria:** unit called "Schwert," also meaning sword
4. **Turkey:** unit called "Red Sheepskin"
5. **Greece:** unit called "Sheepskin"
6. **Sweden:** unit called "Sveaborg"
7. **Switzerland:** unit called "P26"
8. **UK:** unit called "Stay Behind"

Gehlen organization operation areas

tension." The aim was to masquerade as left-wing terrorists and commit terrible atrocities, thus swinging public opinion against the left.

The CIA and their neo-fascist European network created the supposedly communist Red Brigades and instigated acts such as the assassination of the Italian premier Aldo Moro in 1978 (he had been making moves to bring the socialists into government) and the bombing of Bologna train station in 1980.

The neo-fascist network had strong links to the Mafia, the Catholic Church, and the Spanish fascists under Franco, and spread its tentacles into the Vatican and throughout Latin America. One of its aspects was P2, a secret quasi-Masonic lodge that co-ordinated money laundering through the Vatican Bank and underwrote right-wing dictators in South America. P2 conspired with Vatican insiders to kill Pope John Paul I in 1978 (see pages 103–104).

The official line

The anti-fascist conspiracy theory of post-war history is mostly nonsense. It is true that some elements of the Nazi regime were recruited to help the West fight communism, but it would have been inhumane and totally impractical to cast aside totally every individual who had links to the Nazis. The West, led by America, had a higher duty, which was to protect the free world against the evil menace of communism.

People who owe their freedom from the cruel yoke of Stalinist tyranny to the efforts of the CIA and its partners in Europe shouldn't carp and cavil. As for the Italian goings-on, there is no real evidence to link the Red Brigade to the CIA or others, and official Italian investigations back this up. Pope John Paul I died from natural causes.

How paranoid should you be? 56%

The wider fringes of this sprawling conspiracy theory may be doubtful—for instance, while the death of Aldo Moro was tragic and strange, there is little evidence suggesting a CIA role. Equally, however, much of this conspiracy theory is a matter of public record. The CIA did recruit and bankroll many unsavory characters in the post-war years, and senior figures openly admit that the imperatives of anti-communism justified all manner of questionable policies. The after-effects of this twisted agenda linger on today in a legacy of far-right hate groups, while rumours persist that Operation Stay Behind weapons caches remain concealed around Europe.

The Bush-Saudi Connection

The Bush family has close links to the rulers of Saudi Arabia, profiting handsomely. What do the Saudis get in return?

Saudi Arabia (SA) is ruled by the House of Saud. Other prominent Saudi-Arabian dynasties include the Bin Ladens and the Mahfouz family. Global attention has been focused on the Bush-Saudi relationship since the US administration was forced to admit that, in the days following 9/11, special planes evacuated 140 Saudi nationals from the US, including prominent members of the Saudi Royal family and the Bin Laden family, at a time when all flights were supposedly grounded (see pages 56–59 for more on this scandal). It has since come to light that Princess Haifa Al Faisal, wife of the Saudi ambassador and daughter of the late King Faisal, passed hundreds of thousands of dollars to men closely linked to two of the 9/11 hijackers.

What the theorists say

There is a complex web of connections between the Bush family and Saudi ruling families, much of it laid out in Carl Unger's book, *House of Bush, House of Saud*. Unger claims to have traced $1.4 billion in contracts and investments made by leading Saudi families to companies associated with the Bush family and their cronies, including the Carlyle Group, Harken Energy, where George Bush Jr. made his fortune, and Halliburton.

What is in it for the Saudis? Firstly, they have been close friends of two presidents, both of whom launched wars in the region, and were active in helping to shape US policy, sometimes as members of policy-making bodies. Secondly, the Saudis want to avoid any unwelcome scrutiny of their financial misdeeds, such as terrorist funding. The Congressional committee investigating the intelligence failures of 9/11 wanted to make much of this information public but the Bush Administration censored it.

A great deal of attention was paid to the 28 pages of the Congressional report that were ordered classified and blacked-out to the public. People familiar with the missing pages claim that they deal with the SA government's relationship with the 9/11 hijackers. During an interview with CBC News, Eleanor Hill, chief investigator for the Congressional committee, would only confirm that the files dealt with "sources of foreign support for the hijackers."

Despite requests from senators who asked the US government to release the names of SA charities and individuals who were being investigated for funding Al-Qaeda, the Bush Administration refused to place the SA bodies on the terror watch list. Indeed, the day after the request, the names were classified by the Bush Administration. This ensures that the SA friends of Bush will not be called on to face public scrutiny.

There are hints of a darker motive for the Bush-Saudi alliance and its subsequent cover-up—it is suggested they knew that the 9/11 attacks were imminent but let them go ahead (see pages 56–59). They were also jointly planning the Iraq invasion, part of a wider strategy to reshape the Middle East to suit the agenda of the US-Saudi axis.

The official line

There is nothing underhand or illegal about the Bush-Saudi links. Of course, Saudi families invest money in America, and inevitably, some of that cash will be tied up in oil and other companies linked to the Bush family. The other reason for the close relationship is political—SA is one of America's closest Middle Eastern allies, a vital strategic partner in a hostile region. Information about Saudi links to the 9/11 terrorists was censored because it might have embarrassed an important ally.

How paranoid should you be? 70%

When two powerful dynasties such as the Sauds and the Bushes collude, the rest of us should be very worried. The US needs bases in SA and access to its oil and the Sauds depend on American backing to help them maintain their despotic rule. Whether this translates into a 9/11 conspiracy is another matter. Without doubt, however, some shady dealings are being covered up.

Bilderberg Balderdash?

A secret cabal of the European and American elite meets on an annual basis to choose presidents, prime ministers, and direct the course of history.

In 1954, four influential European and American high-flyers started an annual "reunion" of elite and rising political, business, and media figures. The first meeting was at the Bilderberg Hotel in the Netherlands. Remarkably little was known about this group until recently.

What the theorists say

Conspiracy theorists are always looking for the über cabal that controls world events and the Bilderberg group fits the bill. Membership is drawn exclusively from western Europe and North America, and consists mostly of the very rich and powerful. One of the founding members was Polish diplomat and businessman Joseph Retinger, thought to have been a CIA and MI6 stooge. Another was David Rockefeller, scion of the international banking firm accused by many American conspiracy theorists of being the source of all evil.

The location changes each year and there is tight security everywhere as journalists attempting to report on the group have discovered; they can expect to find themselves shadowed by anonymous men in black driving black cars with tinted windows. The fact that any attempts to report on the group's activities have been quashed by Bilderberg's considerable media influence has allowed the group to operate in virtual secrecy for 50 years, despite its list of attendees reading like a Who's Who of post-war Western history.

So what does Bilderberg do? Most importantly, it determines who will take power in America and western Europe. Virtually every American president and British prime minister of the last fifty years attended a Bilderberg meeting early in their career. Obviously the Bilderberg group decides who the future leaders will be, grooms them for power, uses its pervasive network of influence to ensure they get ahead, and uses its control of the media and the economy to ensure their elections. So much for democracy. It doesn't really matter who the electorate votes for anyway, because chances are that both candidates are Bilderbergers.

Bilderberg meetings also help steer the course of world history. For instance, it was at such an assembly that waging a war on Serbia was agreed on, and doubtless it was also here that Bush Snr. and Bush Jr. were given the go-ahead for their Persian Gulf distractions.

The official line

Bilderberg get-togethers were always intended to be informal gatherings of opinion-formers from all parts of the political spectrum and guest lists are carefully balanced. The events are private, not covert. Privacy is essential to allow guests to speak openly and freely. This also accounts for the desire for confidentiality, although there is no active suppression of reports as evidenced by the extensive information available to the public about procedures and guest lists. Security is obviously important given the high-profile guest list.

Bilderberg meetings provide a forum where policy-makers can debate in a non-confrontational atmosphere and discussions then form the background against which policy decisions can be made. The meetings do not decide policy. The steering committee that draws up the guest list has an eye for talent, plus it is often apparent to informed minds who the rising stars of politics and business are likely to be. There is nothing sinister going on and Bilderbergers do not orchestrate their influence to boost the careers of invitees, although inevitably there is a lot of networking.

How paranoid should you be? 50%

Even if we give Bilderberg the benefit of the doubt, and agree that it is a "talking shop" with innocent intent, it is inherently anti-democratic by its very nature, specifically bringing together the (mainly capitalist and very rich) elite to discuss important issues without public "interference." It must be hugely influential, yet the guest list is drawn up from a tiny portion of the population in a tiny portion of the world.

Enron vs the People

Was the Enron scandal simply a case of colossal financial mismanagement or was there something more sinister afoot?

Enron started in 1985 as a small fuel supply company in Houston, Texas, selling and delivering gas to customers. It diversified to become an energy broker and a dealer in the complex financial instruments of the energy market. In 2001 a corporate whistleblower triggered an investigation into the company's finances, which ultimately led to its collapse, delisting it from the stock exchange and triggering the prosecution of several board members, including former chairman Kenneth Lay. Employees and investors collectively lost billions, including their share options and pensions.

What the theorists say

Enron's chief executives conspired to perpetrate a massive fraud against investors and employees with the help of friends in the government and political influence was purchased with massive contributions. This influence allowed the company to grow exponentially before the fraud was discovered and protected the chief culprits in the aftermath.

Enron's rise as the darling of the financial world coincided with a massive deregulation of the energy markets in Texas and America as a whole. This deregulation was forced through by legislators to whom Enron paid out massive contributions, most prominently Texas Governor and later President George W. Bush, a close personal friend of Kenneth Lay, one of his main fundraisers.

The fraud mainly consisted of cooking the books to make it look as if the company's finances were consistently rosy, so that share prices would steadily keep rising. The chief executives who awarded themselves massive share options benefited accordingly in a "managed earnings scam." The books falsely reflected projected profits as current earnings and enormous debts were shifted off the books into shady, unregulated partnerships. For this service, executives often charged the company tens of millions of dollars. When share prices plummeted under the weight of investigation, chief executives mysteriously managed to offload their shares early enough to pocket more massive profits.

Since 2001, more than 30 people have been criminally charged for their dealings with Enron, including former chief executive Jeffrey K. Skilling and accounting chief Richard A. Causey, who have both pleaded not guilty and await trial alongside Lay. Federal prosecutors also investigated an alleged stock sale by Lay's wife just days before the bankruptcy was announced. It is reported that Linda Lay sold 500,000 stocks to net a profit of $1.2 million.

Enron was just one of several companies revealed to have been practicing this sort of fraud—most of them had contributed heavily to politicians of every stripe, but had particularly strong links to the Republicans and to Bush.

The official line

Enron's problems were the fault of a few bad apples. Kenneth Lay was actually in the dark about these shady transactions. As soon as irregularities were revealed, the authorities acted properly and swiftly, bringing a number of executives to justice. Legislation has now been changed to ensure similar scandals do not reoccur.

How paranoid should you be? 52%

Where Wall Street and capitalism are concerned, it is wise to be paranoid. There always have been, and always will be, avaricious frauds, con men, and criminals looking to rip off investors. The Enron scandal and others like it throw light on the disproportionate influence of big business on politics, especially in America, where it almost exclusively funds the increasingly expensive careers of politicians. In return, these companies obtain legislation favorable to them without being hampered by too much regulation. Root and branch campaign reform may be the only way to remove a rotten core.

The New Jerusalem

The religious right, through an organization called The Fellowship, is taking over America, with Bush in the vanguard.

America is one of the most religious countries in the developed world and an increasing number of its citizens are conservative Christians with strong views on abortion, homosexuality, and other cultural issues. There is an ever-growing fringe of fundamentalist Christians with extreme views about instituting a theocracy in America and initiating Armageddon in the Middle East to hasten the Second Coming. Fortunately, the American Constitution guarantees that Church and State be kept separate, right?

What the theorists say

The Christian Right, through its electoral muscle and funding power, increasingly sets the agenda for US politics and society. Some organizations do this in an above-board fashion but others operate like secret societies, recruiting members and peddling influence in underhand, covert ways. One of the scariest of these organizations is The Fellowship (aka The Family), a broad umbrella for a variety of different groups, all with the same philosophy—to evangelize among the rich right-wing and build secret networks of power in order to influence policy and promote their "people" into government. The Fellowship funds expensive digs for senators and congressmen in Washington DC and organizes meetings and think-tanks to browbeat susceptible politicians, businessmen, and media figures (for example, the National Prayer Breakfast). Doug Coe, the leader of The Family, has said, "We work with power where we can, build new power where we can't."

Most disturbingly, The Fellowship uses its network to forge close links between American leaders and shady characters in other parts of the world, such as Indonesian dictator General Suharto, Salvadorean torturer General

Carlos Eugenios Vides Casanova, and Honduran death squad leader General Gustavo Alvarez Martinez. These figures share the same aggressively anti-communist agenda, now transformed into an anti-terror agenda, although both agendas seek the same goal—that of maintaining the status quo in a way that favors big capital and big business (which mainly profits America and its corrupt Third World cronies who prosper from generous backhanders), regardless of the degree of brutality, suppression, and injustice involved. In the warped world of the Christian Right, this equates to doing God's work!

Other Christian Right groups include the Biblical Reconstructionists, who believe in the Bible's literal truth and the need to actively prepare the world for the Second Coming by triggering the Apocalypse if necessary, and Christian Reconstructionists, who want to turn America into a religious dictatorship where abortionists and homosexuals are imprisoned or executed.

These are the groups that selected Bush as a presidential candidate, jockeyed for his nomination, and funded both of his campaigns. As payback, Bush is furthering their reactionary agenda on abortion, homosexuality, and breaking down the Church–State divide, supporting big business, and getting further embroiled with repressive regimes around the world.

The official line
The Christian Right champions a return to more traditional moral values and argues these faith-based policies are exactly what the country needs. The liberal media and faithless intellectual elite, who have for too long set the nation's agenda in opposition to the wishes of the people, try to smear it with lies and distortions, but the Christian Right represents the opinion and will of the majority of Americans.

How paranoid should you be? 77%
Bush has to tread carefully to avoid being seen to trample on the principle of the Church–State divide and to avoid being associated with fringe elements like the Biblical Reconstructionists. But it is well known that right-wing evangelists like Billy Graham and Jerry Falwell have Bush's ear and that he pushes faith-based initiatives, while senior Administration officials like John

Ashcroft, Attorney General during Bush's first term in office, are constantly assaulting the Church–State separation. In a press conference in 2001 Bush called the War on Terror a "crusade," which suggests he sees himself as a sort of holy warrior tested by events like 9/11. It seems unlikely we will ever know the full extent of Fundamentalist influence on the White House and the US government but we should probably be concerned.

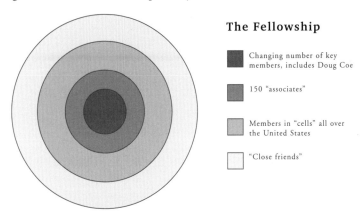

The Fellowship

Changing number of key members, includes Doug Coe

150 "associates"

Members in "cells" all over the United States

"Close friends"

Known Areas of Past and Present Influence of The Fellowship
- Oil industry
- Aerospace industry
- General Soharto, Indonesia
- Senior Chinese officials
- General Carlos Eugenios Vides Casanova, El Salvador
- General Gustavo Alvarez Martinez, Honduras
- Truce in Rwanda

Numerous Guises of The Fellowship
- National Committee for Christian Leadership
- International Christian Leadership
- National Leadership Council
- Fellowship House
- Fellowship Foundation
- National Fellowship Council
- International Foundation

The New Opium Wars

The US and its allies used the War on Terror as a front for the invasion of Afghanistan in order to reinstate the flow of opium from the region.

Under the Soviets, opium production in Afghanistan was severely restricted. In 1989, the mujahideen booted out the Soviets and turned Afghanistan into an opium factory. The Taliban initially increased production but later decided it was immoral and clamped down on it. Since the US invasion, production has rocketed, reaching all-time record levels. Afghanistan now produces around 75 percent of the world's opium, bringing around $3 billion into the country—more than half of its gross domestic product!

What the theorists say

Wherever the US, and in particular the CIA, get involved, drug production and trafficking rockets. This was true in 1960s and 1970s Indochina, Afghanistan in the 1980s and 1990s, and Latin America since the 1980s. Nowadays it is once again true of Afghanistan. What's more, UN and US researchers reported an explosion of trafficking and drug abuse in Iraq in the wake of the US invasion. Is this a coincidence? Absolutely not. The CIA has for decades been a vast state conspiracy, raising illegal funds beyond government oversight and spending them to further its agenda around the world. How best to do this? By facilitating the production and trafficking of narcotics, the world's third most valuable commodity in terms of international trade after oil and arms.

The sums involved in heroin trafficking alone are staggering. While Afghan farmers took home about $1.5–2 billion from their poppy crop in 2003, the end value of the heroin produced from it is conservatively estimated at $60 billion, although it is probably higher. This means that the middle men are pocketing over $55 billion a year in the form of money laundered through the world's banks and other "legitimate" companies. The CIA has even set up a vast network of front companies and banks to do just this, helping it to process the funds that it accrues from protecting/taxing drug smugglers and also getting directly involved (for more on the cocaine angle, see pages 23–24).

The US wanted to invade Afghanistan to restore the cultivation of poppy fields and restart the flood of opium trafficking that it, in collusion with its allies in the Pakistan intelligence service and the Afghan warlords, has controlled ever since it kicked out the Soviets. During the 1990s, the US turned a blind eye to opium trafficking by the Taliban and Al-Qaeda. When they became enemies, it needed to intervene to reinstate more direct control of the trade and its profits. The US pays lip service to the War on Terror, but in reality, it is happy for disadvantaged portions of society to drug themselves into oblivion, while agencies like the CIA simultaneously pocket the proceeds of drug trafficking and any anti-drugs funding.

The official line

Fighting opium production in Afghanistan is a major priority and the US supports the vigorous efforts of the democratic Afghan regime to stamp out poppy cultivation. It is absurd to suggest that the CIA, or any other US government agencies, condone drug trafficking, let alone profit by it.

How paranoid should you be? 13%

Rogue elements and poorly supervised CIA assets are almost certainly involved in drug trafficking but it seems unlikely that the CIA as an institution actively engages in it. It is, however, widely acknowledged that the US has let control of the drugs trade take a back seat to building alliances in the War on Terror. As Rensselaer Lee, an expert on the international drug trade, told a Senate committee in 2003, "To build these alliances, unfortunately we've had to make some arrangements, compromises with people who . . . may be protecting the drug trade." Intentionally or not, the US has created a narco-state that will spread drugs, crime, and misery throughout the region and the world for decades to come.

Lone Nuts?

Two men were convicted of the Oklahoma bombing, but there is evidence that a white supremacist gang was involved and of a political cover-up.

On April 19, 1995, a truck bomb exploded before the Alfred P. Murrah federal building in Oklahoma City, killing 168 people. In 2001, Timothy McVeigh, who was convicted for having parked the truck, was executed. In March 2004, Terry Nichols was convicted as his fellow conspirator. By most accounts, Nichols stayed home the day of the bombing. McVeigh insisted he did the bombing all by himself, although dozens of eyewitnesses identified other persons on the scene and in his company in the days preceding and on the day of the bombing. No such persons have ever been charged in a court of law. The prosecution sought the death penalty but Nichols got life without parole. The bombing was the worst act of domestic terrorism in US history.

What the theorists say

There are several holes in the official story, mainly uncovered by investigative reporters. For starters, there was more to the explosion than meets the eye. Investigative reporter J. D. Cash used seismograph evidence to prove there were two explosions. The FBI had to admit they had been storing a disarmed but fully fuelled Stinger missile in the building.

More disturbingly, there is much evidence that McVeigh was involved with a white supremacist gang of bank robbers called the Aryan Republican Army (ARA), probably as a getaway driver. Despite a lack of witness testimony and contradictory evidence, Nichols was convicted of robbing a gun dealer who had helped fund the bombing and of stealing the blasting caps used to make the bomb. In fact, the evidence suggests these crimes were carried out by the ARA, since identical blasting caps were found in an ARA hideout, while the gang also possessed a driver's licence bearing the alias of the gun dealer who was robbed.

Pete Langan and Richard Guthrie, leading lights in the ARA, have both claimed involvement in the Oklahoma bombing (the latter via a posthumous manuscript). Those familiar with the story agree that McVeigh would have been incapable of planning, funding, or executing such a complex plot, yet the authorities had him executed, tried to get Nichols executed, and ignored the evidence against the ARA.

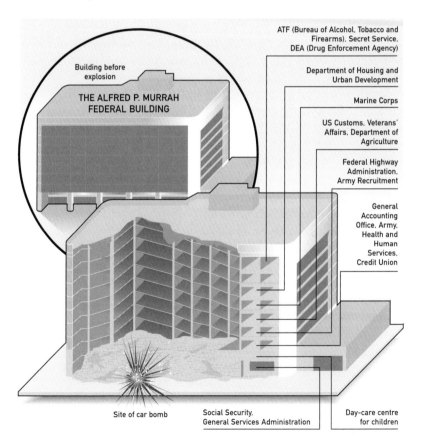

Building before explosion

THE ALFRED P. MURRAH FEDERAL BUILDING

ATF (Bureau of Alcohol, Tobacco and Firearms), Secret Service, DEA (Drug Enforcement Agency)

Department of Housing and Urban Development

Marine Corps

US Customs, Veterans' Affairs, Department of Agriculture

Federal Highway Administration, Army Recruitment

General Accounting Office, Army, Health and Human Services, Credit Union

Site of car bomb

Social Security, General Services Administration

Day-care centre for children

Langan was probably recruited by the FBI during the 1990s to spy on militia groups, so there was embarrassment about these links and an investigation would have revealed unpalatable truths about the close ties between religious right and militia groups on the one hand, and state and federal authorities on the other.

The official line

To begin with, no one is suppressing anything: The FBI have admitted that some leads were not followed up properly, and in March 2004 they announced that they were reopening the investigation into the bombing. Notwithstanding, the ARA tale lacks credibility. It was concocted by Nichols's defense team to try to get him off, and the judge in the case deemed it to be lacking credibility—and he should know best.

Nichols's sentencing, like McVeigh's, was in the hands of the jury, and not the authorities (since the death penalty was involved), and he was not sentenced to death. Neither he nor McVeigh have ever mentioned anyone else's involvement. Langan, on the other hand, is known to have serious mental issues (he was a cross-dresser whose desire for a sex change conflicted with his fundamentalist views, leading to severe mental disturbances).

How paranoid should you be? 70%

There's obviously more to the Oklahoma bombing than meets the eye, and it seems likely that McVeigh and Nichols were part of a white supremacist gang that was responsible. Whether there has been a cover-up or simply a stuff-up by the authorities is less clear. But then much in the murky world of American far-right parapolitics is disturbingly unclear.

The WMD Deception

The real reasons for going to war
with Iraq had nothing to do with WMD
and everything to do with the Neocon
project for a new American century.

In the build-up to the 2003 US-led invasion of Iraq, much was made of Iraq's weapons of mass destruction (WMD). Saddam Hussein supposedly had nuclear, chemical, and biological weapons capability, and there was a clear and present danger that he might use them. Since the invasion, it has come to light there were no such weapons lurking in Iraqi territory.

What the theorists say

The issue of WMD was a grand deception designed to mobilize public support and construct the case for war. In fact, deceit was going on at two different levels.

Firstly, the deception of the US by Iranian intelligence using Ahmed Chalabi, head of the Iraqi National Congress (INC), as an agent of disinformation. Chalabi was an influential Iraqi exile whose close links to US intelligence dated back to the first Gulf War. When Bush came to office in 2000, he brought with him the Neoconservatives, radical right-wing ideologs who believed in American interventionism and who were burning to invade Iraq. The Neocons needed to build the case for war and Chalabi proved to be the perfect tool. His extensive network of contacts supplied a stream of Saddam regime defectors who told the Neocons exactly what they wanted to hear: that Saddam was amassing WMD in Iraq. In return, the Neocons at the Pentagon funded Chalabi and his INC to the tune of millions of dollars.

Unfortunately, Chalabi's links with Iranian intelligence predated his US affiliation, and it seems likely the Iranians used him to feed the Neocons a stream of disinformation that would encourage America to do Iran's dirty work by removing Saddam and setting up a new Shia-based regime in which Iranian influence was uppermost. The CIA and the State Department knew about Chalabi's Iranian connection and tried to warn the Pentagon, but the response of Donald Rumsfeld, Neocon Secretary of Defense, was simply to set up his own, in-house intelligence agency, the Office of Special Plans, specifically tasked with gathering intelligence to support the Neocon case.

Why were the Neocons so easily deceived? Probably because they were willing to be deceived, if it helped to further their dreams of an American world order. In this utopia, American force would remodel the Middle East by invading Iraq and Iran, if necessary, thus safeguarding American access to oil and spreading US values through the rest of the region.

Accordingly, the second level of WMD deception was the Neocon deception before the American people by any and all means necessary: using 9/11 as a pretext for the Iraq invasion; making false links between Saddam and Bin Laden; falsely insisting that Iraq was a sponsor of terror; and, of course, touting Saddam's possession of WMD.

In the wake of the invasion, the deception was unmasked. No WMD were found and Chalabi's Iranian connections were uncovered when the Americans intercepted an Iranian intelligence message discussing how Chalabi had passed them top-secret US intelligence.

The official line

Intelligence failures over WMD were a genuine mistake, made not just by the Americans but also by the British, French, Germans, and everyone else involved. Chalabi has been the victim of a turf war between the Neocon Pentagon and the old guard in the CIA and the US State Department. A report from the American military insisted that intelligence supplied by Chalabi's INC has been of generally good quality and saved US lives. American motives for the invasion of Iraq were pure and intent on "freeing the Iraqi people from tyranny" and remain so. There is nothing sinister about the willingness to use force in the interest of spreading democracy to bring down despotic dictators.

Pre-invasion Map of Supposed WMD Sites, According to US Government Sources

1. Al Jasira
2. Mosul
3. Saddam airbase
4. Ash Sharqat
5. At Tuz airbase
6. Al Qa'im
7. Ar Rashidiyah
8. Qadisiyah airbase
9. Petrochemical-3 center
10. Saad airbase
11. Akashat
12/13. Murasana airfield
14. Al Walid airbase
15. Al Tabaat airfield
16. Al Furat
17. Al Atheer
18. Tatha airbase

31. Al Nebai
32. Mutasim airbase
33. At Tarmiyah
34. Al Mansurlyah
35. Kham Bani Saad airfield
36. Taji bridge
37. Fudhaliyah
38. Al Kindi
39. Daura
40. Salman Pak
41. Tuwaitha
42. Al Aziziyah
43. Abu Obeydi airbase
44. Al Maymunah
45. Al Nasiriyah/Khamisiyah

19. Al Muhammadiyat
20. Al Muhammadiyat
21. Airfield 37
22. Al Muthanna
23. Fallujah lll
24. Zaghareet
25. Fallujah ll
26. Al Fallujah forest
27. Tammuz airbase
28. Tigris canal
29. Al Hakam
30. Ukhaydir

☢ Nuclear facilities
● Biological warfare-related sites
Chemical warfare-related facilities

How paranoid should you be? 99%

Colin Powell, the man who took the intelligence evidence of WMD in Iraq to the UN in order to argue that a resolution be passed, has since admitted that there were no WMD. With the precedent set, we should be wary of more deception operations.

9/11

Bush and his advisors either planned the attacks or let them happen in order to secure their hold on power and increase defense spending.

On September 11, 2001, jet planes slammed into the Twin Towers of the World Trade Center in New York, killing nearly 3,000 people. Shortly afterward, a third plane crashed into the Pentagon, while a fourth never hit its intended target because it was brought down by passenger action. In the wake of the terrorist bombings, the US instituted massive curbs on civil liberties, dramatically increased funding for intelligence agencies and the military, went to war in Afghanistan and Iraq, and voted Bush into office for a second term.

What the theorists say

The main thrust of 9/11 conspiracy theories is that Bush and his cabinet either planned the attacks or knew about them to some degree and deliberately let them go ahead. Following is a quick tour through some of the suggestive evidence.

Official investigations have proven that there were numerous general and specific warnings leading up to the attacks. A good example is the July 5, 2001 briefing by top White House counterterrorism official Richard Clarke in which he warned, "Something really spectacular is going to happen here, and it's going to happen soon."

There is evidence that FBI investigations into some of the hijackers were squashed from on high in the weeks preceding 9/11. There is also proof that the government interfered with investigations post-9/11—for instance, by spiriting top Saudis, including members of the Bin Laden family, out of the US immediately afterward (see The Bush-Saudi Connection, pages 39–40).

Several high-ranking officials seem to have been mysteriously forewarned. Then Attorney General John Ashcroft was warned not to take commercial airlines from July 2001. San Francisco mayor Willie Brown was advised not to board commercial flights on the morning of the attacks. A group of top Pentagon officials cancelled plane trips, apparently acting on a warning received on the night of September 10.

The US Air Force did not send any planes until well after the attacks. This delay has not been satisfactorily explained. Many commentators are skeptical that the damage to the Pentagon was commensurate with being hit by an airliner and suggest it was a missile attack.

Evidence surrounding the alleged hijackers is riddled with problems. A lot of incriminating items, such as the "luggage, letters, and suicide bomber kits" found in the hijackers' cars, look suspiciously planted. Other aspects, such as testimonies that the hijackers regularly liked to visit strip clubs and take cocaine (which goes against the image the government wanted to propagate) have been suspiciously ignored, as have the suggestive links between some of the hijackers and US intelligence and its allies.

Why would the Bush Administration want to carry out such a terrible act? The President and his cabinet have definitely benefited from the atrocity. Before 9/11, Bush was a lame duck president struggling to escape questions about his fraudulent election and his Administration was beset by scandals such as the Enron debacle.

On a wider scale, the vast military-security complex was also suffering. Having spent 50 years exaggerating the threat posed by the Soviets to justify its consumption of more than 50 percent of US tax revenues, it was now faced with a world where there was no headline-grabbing "bad guy," and no clear and present danger.

After 9/11, Bush was a wartime president-hero and it became unpatriotic to question his motives. He was able to secure backing for two controversial wars that were integral to the Neocon program (see The WMD Deception, pages 53–55) and which enriched companies such as Halliburton; the scandals that had threatened to engulf him were relegated to the backburner; the media became compliant and unchallenging; and a second term in office

Map of the Events of 9/11

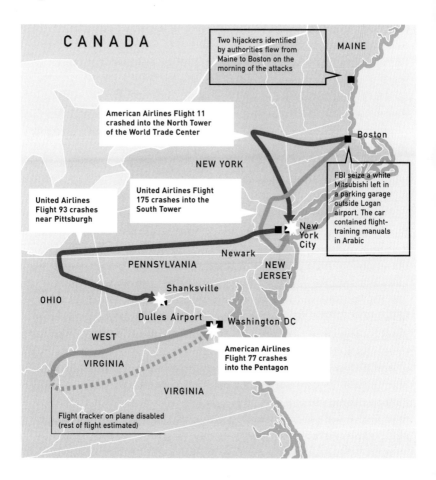

CANADA

MAINE

Two hijackers identified by authorities flew from Maine to Boston on the morning of the attacks

American Airlines Flight 11 crashed into the North Tower of the World Trade Center

Boston

NEW YORK

FBI seize a white Mitsubishi left in a parking garage outside Logan airport. The car contained flight-training manuals in Arabic

United Airlines Flight 93 crashes near Pittsburgh

United Airlines Flight 175 crashes into the South Tower

New York City

Newark

PENNSYLVANIA

NEW JERSEY

Shanksville

OHIO

Dulles Airport

Washington DC

WEST

American Airlines Flight 77 crashes into the Pentagon

VIRGINIA

VIRGINIA

Flight tracker on plane disabled (rest of flight estimated)

was secured on the back of it all. The military-security complex had found a new crusade to replace the Cold War: the War on Terror.

Many people find it impossible to believe that a government could be capable of such a monstrous act. Since 9/11, the Bush Administration has shown its true colors, practicing massive deception and sanctioning torture and terror. There is also plenty of pre-9/11 evidence to support the unthinkable. For instance, the claim that Roosevelt knew about the imminent attack on Pearl Harbor but let it go ahead to mobilize public opinion for going to war, just as Bush has done in the build up to 9/11, seems more plausible than ever. The US military fabricated an attack on a US boat in the Gulf of Tonkin incident as a pretext for massively escalated involvement in Vietnam. We also now know about Operation Northwoods, an elaborate plan drawn up in 1962 as an excuse for the invasion of Cuba. The plan called for assassination and terror attacks against Cuban émigrés and US cities. The Kennedy Administration apparently scotched the plan. In other words, it should not be too difficult to believe that the worst is possible and that the Bush junta had motive, means, and opportunity.

The official line
Suggestions that the government knew about or in any way colluded with the terrorists are ridiculous and offensive in the extreme. Congress has fully investigated the events of 9/11 and concluded, in a thorough and publicly available report, that, while there were serious errors of judgment, no one individual was culpable. A major event of this type inevitably attracts conspiracy theorists but the US government at the time was as much taken by surprise and appalled by the violence and inhumanity of the attacks as were the inhabitants of New York City and indeed the rest of the nation.

How paranoid should you be? 23%
No one can deny that Bush and his supporters have made the most of the opportunity that 9/11 presented. But could a conspiracy of such magnitude really be covered up, and if so, for how long? Perhaps the most disturbing part of the whole scenario has been the remarkable quiescence of mainstream media and its reluctance to challenge the unconvincing official version.

Titanic Mix-up

It wasn't the Titanic that sank in the North Atlantic but her sister ship the Olympic, as part of an elaborate insurance fraud.

In 1907, the White Star Line shipping company commissioned two of the greatest liners ever built, the *Olympic*, and her even more impressive sister ship, the *Titanic*.

On the night of April 14 to 15, 1912, during her maiden voyage across the Atlantic, the *Titanic* hit an iceberg, puncturing several of the special watertight compartments that were supposed to make her unsinkable. Equipped with too few lifeboats, the mighty ship went down with 1,523 souls on board. The *Olympic* went on to have a successful 30-year career carrying passengers across the Atlantic and served with distinction as a troop carrier during World War II.

What the theorists say

The myth of the *Titanic* was concocted to hide the fact that the White Star Line had managed to drown more than 1,500 passengers in a botched insurance fraud.

The true story begins in 1911 when the *Olympic* collided with a British warship off the coast of Southampton, suffering significant damage and leaving the shipping company with a financial and logistical headache. The Navy insisted they were not to blame so the insurers would not cough up. The *Olympic* would have to be jerry-rigged to get to the yards at Belfast (the only place with big enough docks), where the *Titanic* was being prepared for her April launch. The *Olympic* was almost irreparably damaged and trying to repair her would set back the maiden voyage of the *Titanic*, causing massive embarrassment and significant outlay in refunds. Meanwhile, every day that the *Olympic* spent out of action also meant lost revenue.

The owners decided to perpetrate a switch. The ships were very similar, except for some cosmetic differences, so the shipwrights were put to work altering the *Titanic*'s deck and porthole layout to look like the *Olympic*, and vice versa. Two months later, the new "*Olympic*" slipped out of Belfast to begin her long and fruitful career.

The battered ship, now rechristened as the *Titanic*, was patched up just enough to get her out of port in time for her "maiden" voyage. The plan was to sail her to the mid-Atlantic, rendezvous with some rescue ships, announce a bogus fault or accident, and safely offload all the passengers before scuttling the ship and claiming the insurance money. But the ship struck an iceberg, or possibly one of the rescue ships, and went down with massive loss of life. Desperate to cover up their crime, the White Star Line created the myth that endures to this day.

The official line

Practically everyone in the Belfast shipyard would have known what had gone on, yet mysteriously no one ever spoke up about what would have been the crime of the century. The two ships were too different to pass off as one another and exploration of the wreck of the *Titanic* proved it was the genuine article.

How paranoid should you be? 0%

It might make a good yarn but this fishy theory holds no water.

Route of Olympic
Route of Titanic

Olympic
1. Oct 20, 1910: launched
   June 14, 1911: maiden voyage

2. Sept 20, 1911: hit HMS Hawke in Solent. Went to Belfast for repairs
   Nov 30, 1911: resumes normal service
   Feb 1912: overhaul in Belfast and new propeller fitted
   1912–1913: returned to Belfast for six months for safety rebuild
   April 2, 1913: resumes service

Titanic
3. May 31, 1911: launched

4. April 2, 1912: sea trials— heads for Southampton

5. April 10, 1912: leaves Southampton for Cherbourg and then on to Queenstown, Ireland

6. April 11, 1912: leaves Ireland for New York

A Right Royal Cover-up?

Jack the Ripper was a Royal surgeon who murdered to conceal a shameful Royal secret at Queen Victoria's request.

In 1888, Britain and the civilized world were shocked by a series of brutal murders in London's Whitechapel area. Five prostitutes were killed by a figure dubbed "Jack the Ripper" by the popular press. He was never caught and the case remains unsolved.

What the theorists say

Numerous authors have supplied alternative hypotheses. The most incredible theory is that detailed by Stephen Knight in his book *Jack the Ripper: The Final Solution*. The victims were all prostitutes blackmailing Prince Albert

Victor (second in line to the throne) about his secret marriage to a Catholic prostitute named Annie Crook, whom he had got pregnant and from whom he had caught syphilis. To hush this up, Queen Victoria asked Sir William Gull, the Royal surgeon, to lobotomize

Left An illustration from 1888 showing police discovering the body of one of Jack the Ripper's victims, Catherine Eddowes.

Annie and kill the blackmailers. The brutality of the murders was intended as some sort of Masonic warning to an occult group. The Metropolitan Police Commissioner, Sir Charles Warren, also a Mason, helped cover Gull's tracks and ordered the erasure of a Masonic message about "Juwes" (a reference to mythical Masonic figures) from the wall at one of the murder scenes.

Knight's theory hinges on a few key facts. The speed and skill displayed in the butchering shows that the Ripper must have had some knowledge of anatomy and experience of using a surgical knife. Most victims were prostitutes who lived within one city block of one another. The incompetence of the police investigation and the failure to catch the murderer suggest a cover-up. The cryptic message on the wall was indeed erased on Warren's orders. The chilling nature of the murders referenced brutal Masonic rituals. Gull was identified as the murderer by psychic Robert James Lees who later questioned Gull's wife. She confirmed her husband had returned with blood-soaked clothes one night.

The official line

Much of Knight's story is pure fabrication. Prince Albert Victor is now thought to have been homosexual and died of influenza. Annie Crook did exist but there is no evidence she was lobotomized. The victims did live close to one another, but then so did large numbers of people in overcrowded London slums. Did they even know one another? The police investigation was unsuccessful because of the limitations of Victorian forensic science. Warren ordered the graffiti to be removed to avoid sparking an anti-Semitic riot, but was it even written by the murderer? There are no Masonic rituals resembling the murders. Lees did exist but he never questioned Gull's wife.

How paranoid should you be? 1%

The British Royal family do have a long history of involvement in conspiracies but Knight's tale is pure fiction. The murders were the work of a deviant, not the product of a planned conspiracy. Even today, serial killers are hard to catch; before forensic sciences, it would have been impossible to track down such a figure in the anonymous slums of Victorian London.

The Knights Templar and the Bloodline of Jesus

What did the mysterious medieval warrior monks discover in the bowels of Solomon's Temple and who still protects their secret today?

Founded in the twelfth century to protect pilgrims to the Holy Land, the Knights Templar (Poor Knights of Christ and of the Temple) took their name from the location of their headquarters next to the ruins of Solomon's Temple

in Jerusalem. Grants of land and money and expertise in banking made the order rich and powerful until its destruction at the hands of the French monarchy and the Pope in 1312.

What the theorists say

Excavating the ruins of the Temple, the Knights discovered the Holy Grail, only it was not a physical object but a shocking revelation that undermined the very basis of the established Church. Jesus had survived the crucifixion and gone on to father children by Mary Magdalene. This divine bloodline had ruled most of Europe as the

Left Illustration from 1250 of a member of the Knights Templar, with hands bound.

Merovingians but now depended on the guardianship of the Templars to survive and assume its rightful role in fighting the forces of darkness. This and other discoveries—for example, the talking head of John the Baptist and the secrets of monumental masonry—were the true basis of Templar wealth, power, and influence, and also led them to follow a new version of Christianity with strange rites, such as spitting on the cross and worshipping heads.

Threatened by the Templar secret, the Church colluded with the jealous French monarchy to destroy the Order and steal its wealth, accusing them of devil worship, homosexuality, and suppressing them with great cruelty. Forewarned, the Templars' mighty fleet fled with the Order's most valued treasures, setting up a new base in Scotland around the Rosslyn Chapel built by the Sinclair family. Here the Templars lived on, eventually founding the Freemasons and other secret societies, and guiding the discovery of America and later the American and French Revolutions. Meanwhile, the Bloodline of Jesus lived on under the guardianship of these new orders, in particular, a French outfit called the Priory of Sion, whose members included prominent artists, intellectuals, and leaders, from Leonardo da Vinci to Victor Hugo. This global network of Templar-descended secret societies guides much of world history from the shadows.

The official line

"Proper" historians scoff at most of this tale. It is true that the Templars were suppressed in 1312, and that lurid allegations were made against them, but this was typical of heresy trials at the time. There are no records of the Templars ever having discovered anything in the ruins of the Temple or elsewhere. They had no fleet and there is no evidence that treasures were smuggled out. However, the Order did live on in a diminished form in Scotland and Portugal, and while they may have played a role in Portuguese voyages of discovery, there is no evidence of a significant role in Scottish history. Since the eighteenth century, branches of Masonry and other secret societies have often claimed to be descended from the Templars. This is romantic fantasy and has no basis in fact. The Priory of Sion is basically a fiction invented by a French con man and promoted by modern-day alternative archaeologists to help shift books (the latest being *The Da Vinci Code*), as is the entire story about the Bloodline of Christ.

How paranoid should you be? 3½

An entire industry of books, documentaries, and even tourism has evolved around the Templar mystery but it is a house of cards. The "evidence" for most of the conspiracy theory is simply a chain of suppositions. There is, however, a core of fascinating historical mystery. The Templars genuinely did have many strange practices and beliefs, doubtless borrowed from time spent in the Middle East during the Crusades. They may be early examples of the mystical tradition of Gnostic Christianity which, as an intellectual movement, went on to inspire the Enlightenment and the French and American Revolutions.

Above A meeting of a branch of the Knights Templar around 1128. Seated in the middle of the picture is the Grand Master.

The Jubilee Plot

The British secret services nearly got
Queen Victoria blown up in a fake
terrorist plot instigated to discredit
the Irish Home Rule movement.

In the 1880s, charismatic politician Charles Parnell was gaining popular
support for his Home Rule for Ireland movement. On the eve of Queen
Victoria's Golden Jubilee, the police revealed a dastardly plot by Irish-
American secret society Clan na Gael (Fenian Brotherhood) to blow up
Westminster Abbey with the Queen and Cabinet inside it, a plot that was
linked by letters to Parnell. There was public outrage and the Parnellite cause
suffered great damage as a result. Not long afterward, however, the letters
were revealed to be fakes forged by Dublin journalist Richard Pigott and sold
to the *Times* newspaper. Suspicion about the whole affair deepened.
"General" Francis Millen, the alleged ringleader of the plot, had mysteriously
escaped capture and fled to New York. He was found murdered after being
offered a princely sum to return to Britain to testify.

What the theorists say

The British secret services set up the Jubilee Plot as a provocation to
discredit Parnell and the Home Rule cause. They recruited Millen in
Mexico, paid him wages, encouraged him to set up the plot, and had a
journalist cook up letters implicating Parnell. It apparently did not occur to
them that the angry Fenians involved would actually want to go through
with the plan. Two terrorists armed with explosives only just missed blowing
up Westminster Abbey and Queen Victoria because the passenger ship they
were expecting to catch across the Atlantic unexpectedly turned out to be
fully booked.

Undaunted, the secret services revealed the plot and the compliant
press stirred up public outrage even as the authorities were spiriting the

"wanted" Millen to safety. When there was danger that he might talk, they had him killed.

The official line

At the time, the full story never emerged because a sort of Victorian Warren Commission was appointed to ensure it was suppressed. More recently, however, newly released government papers revealed the shabby story in full as pieced together by Christy Campbell in his book, *Fenian Fire*. The official attitude is to dismiss the whole affair as ancient history. That was then, the argument goes, and this sort of thing could never happen now.

How paranoid should you be? 79%

British parliamentary oversight of the intelligence services has probably improved, but official placation rings hollow when you survey the list of (known) black operations perpetrated by the secret services in the years since. In 1924, for instance, a forged note known as the "Zinoviev Letter" made bogus links between the Comintern, the organization encouraging international revolution, and the fledgling Labour Party, while 50 years later, MI5 employed

similar tactics to plant stories about links between Labour and the IRA. On an international scale, the plot bears comparison with such deception operations as the Gulf of Tonkin incident and Operation Northwoods (see page 59).

Left The parade makes its way through London toward Westminster Abbey for Queen Victoria's Golden Jubilee, on June 22, 1887.

Bohemian Grove

The global elite hold regular covert gatherings in a top-secret location to engage in pagan rituals and determine the course of world politics.

The Bohemian Club was formed by bored San Francisco journalists in 1872 or 1873 (sources differ) but soon became the preserve of the rich elite when they purchased a redwood forest in Northern California known as Bohemian Grove. This was the site of an annual camping get-together, where 2,000 exclusively male business, political, and media leaders came to relax, let their hair down, and forget about their worries. "Camp" is something of a euphemism as "Grovers" hardly roughed it and the campsites were equipped with bars, hot tubs and the like. The club's motto was "weaving spiders come not here" (talking shop is banned).

What the theorists say

Bohemian Grove attendees have included all the major Republican politicians of the last 80 years (including all US presidents since 1923), together with *Fortune*'s top 500 business leaders, heads of global financial bodies, such as the World Bank, select foreign leaders, and arch-conspiracy figures, such as Henry Kissinger. They urinate in the open, dress up in drag, fornicate with prostitutes, and stage a pagan ritual where an effigy is sacrificed to a giant stone owl (Moloch); more extreme conspiracy theorists claim that the effigy is sometimes replaced by a real person. An article in a local community newspaper, *Santa Rosa Sun*, reported on human sacrifices of the Moloch Cult bring practiced at the Grove and in the mid 1980s there were rumors of murders in remote parts of the property. According to one witness who claims to have been an observer and near victim, the inner sanctum of the Grove contains an Underground Lounge, a Leather Room, a Dark Room, and a Necrophilia Room.

More importantly, attendees lobby furiously, peddle influence, choose presidents and Supreme Court judges, decide where to launch wars, and generally carve up the world. It was here that the Manhattan Project, which led to the development of the atom bomb, was conceived and it is here that big business cozies up to politics to arrange lucrative government contracts and determine spending priorities—for instance, starting wars from which the military-industrial complex can profit.

The official line

The rituals are simply sub-Masonic play-acting. The effigy represents "Dull Care," which is symbolically burned so a lot of stressed-out men can enjoy a fortnight's break with a bit of amateur dramatics. There are speeches on current topics of interest and there may be some networking but it is entirely harmless fun.

How paranoid should you be? 24%

The weird antics at Bohemian Grove probably represent nothing more a chance for America's elite to relive the summer camp frolics of their youth. But it is inherently undemocratic for the (exclusively male) American ruling class and the world to hobnob in secrecy with each other. For instance, George W. Bush regularly hung out here with John J. O'Connor, husband of Supreme Court Justice Sandra Day O'Connor, who, as a woman, was not allowed to attend the Grove but whose crucial vote won him the 2000 election. Other attendees have included most members of George W.'s White House staff, including Dick Cheney, Donald Rumsfeld, and Colin Powell. Equally suspicious is the remarkable reluctance of mainstream media to report on this bizarre convocation.

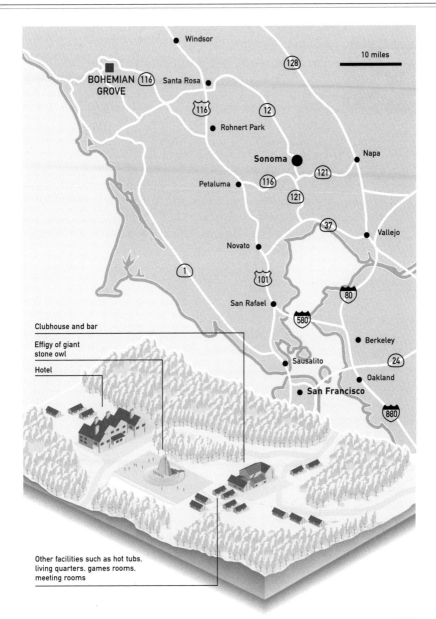

Windsor

10 miles

128

BOHEMIAN 116 Santa Rosa
GROVE

116

12

Rohnert Park

Sonoma ●   Napa

121

Petaluma   116

121

37

Vallejo

Novato

1   101

80

San Rafael

580

Clubhouse and bar   Berkeley

Effigy of giant   24
stone owl

Hotel   Sausalito   Oakland

San Francisco

880

Other facilities such as hot tubs,
living quarters, games rooms,
meeting rooms

Skull and Bones

`This secret college fraternity controls America through its role in drug trafficking, the intelligence services, and world trade.`

Skull and Bones (S&B) is one of several very exclusive secret societies at Yale University. Founded in 1832 as an American version of the fraternities popular in German universities at the time, S&B "taps" 15 new male members each year and initiates them at the society's headquarters, a building known as "the Tomb," in a quasi-Masonic ceremony. Bonesmen are expected to maintain strict secrecy about their membership but it is known that previous Bonesmen have included several presidents (including George W. Bush) and many other major figures in American history.

What the theorists say

By building a secret network of elite power brokers and inculcating them with a morbid and anti-democratic philosophy, S&B constantly renews the foundations of a corrupt Illuminati-style conspiracy against the general public. From early in its history, S&B has been dogged by controversy: for instance, a college paper in 1873 railed against the society's "criminal" influence. The power of the Bonesmen, however, has endured and even grown. During the nineteenth century, S&B tapped a stream of scions from the elite families governing America's politics and trade, starting a trend of links to the American intelligence community and drug trafficking in the form of opium trading. Is this more than a coincidence, given suspicions about the CIA's role in modern trafficking (see Is the CIA Peddling Drugs?, pages 23–24 and The New Opium Wars, pages 48–49)?

The elite family connection survives today, particularly with the Bushes; George W. Bush is a third-generation Bonesman. His grandfather, Bonesman Prescott Bush, was heavily involved in financing Nazi industry. It is alleged that

S&B was founded as the chapter of a German college secret society, leading to accusations of long-standing links to Germanic nationalism and fascism.

A deeper criticism of S&B is that its central philosophy is a morbid preoccupation with death. Does this in any way relate to its strong influence on the CIA and the nation's military-industrial complex since at least four Ministers of War have been Bonesmen? Or is S&B a front for something even more sinister—an evil master plan to control world history? Central to this theory is the idea that while people are seemingly offered a choice, both options are actually controlled by S&B. The most obvious example is the 2004 US presidential election, where both candidates, George W. Bush and John Kerry, were Bonesmen.

The official line

S&B is probably no more than a glorified fraternity, somewhere for the "boys" to drink and dress up. If half of what was said about S&B were true, then nobody in a position of power in the US could emerge from any other background. Yet most of the nation's elite come from other schools and are not members of secret societies. Also, given the pool from which S&B draws, it is hardly surprising that its alumni include prominent politicians and business leaders. Families such as the Bushes or Kerrys have a long tradition of public service and their scions would have traveled a similar path whether or not they were tapped for S&B.

How paranoid should you be? 31%

The more lurid allegations of Nazi links and death worshipping can probably be discounted, but S&B does exist, many of the most powerful men in the White House went to Yale and confess to being Bonesmen, and they refuse to discuss any details about what went on in the clandestine club or how membership affects the powerful elite today. If the aim of S&B is to build up a network of influence among the highest echelons of US power from a tiny pool of privileged men, we should all be more than a little paranoid.

What Happened to TWA Flight 800?

A jumbo jet was blown out of the sky by a US Navy missile but a conspiracy and smear campaign has covered up the truth to this day.

Shortly after takeoff on July 17, 1996, TWA flight 800 from New York to Paris exploded in mid-air with the loss of all 230 passengers and crew. Eyewitness reports widely quoted in the media suggested that a missile had struck the plane but the authorities hastily put their own theory forward: a spark had ignited fuel vapor in an empty tank. Even though a four-year investigation was largely inconclusive, it managed to come down in favor of the "official" explanation. The CIA helped explain why witnesses might have thought they saw a missile and explained that witnesses were misled by the sudden change in trajectory of the plane's fuselage after the explosion which looked like a missile streaking across the sky.

What the theorists say

Compelling evidence suggests that the US Navy was testing missiles in the area, having been assured that all air traffic would be flying above a minimum safety ceiling. TWA 800, however, was flying at just 13,000 feet and fell victim to "friendly fire." The authorities embarked on a cover-up operation, scared of the scandal that would follow a revelation of the truth.

Dissatisfied with the official explanation, respected independent investigators compiled a convincing case. Dozens of eyewitness reports clearly state that a streak was seen leaving the surface of the ocean and hitting the plane, only after which did a different streak move in the fashion described by the official report. The physical evidence obtained includes what look like incendiary pellets (a common component of missile warheads) in victims'

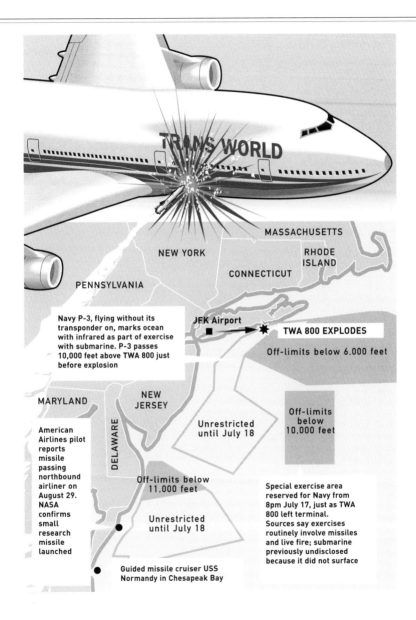

MASSACHUSETTS

NEW YORK

RHODE ISLAND

CONNECTICUT

PENNSYLVANIA

Navy P-3, flying without its transponder on, marks ocean with infrared as part of exercise with submarine. P-3 passes 10,000 feet above TWA 800 just before explosion

JFK Airport

TWA 800 EXPLODES

Off-limits below 6,000 feet

MARYLAND

NEW JERSEY

DELAWARE

Off-limits below 10,000 feet

American Airlines pilot reports missile passing northbound airliner on August 29. NASA confirms small research missile launched

Unrestricted until July 18

Off-limits below 11,000 feet

Unrestricted until July 18

Special exercise area reserved for Navy from 8pm July 17, just as TWA 800 left terminal. Sources say exercises routinely involve missiles and live fire; submarine previously undisclosed because it did not surface

Guided missile cruiser USS Normandy in Chesapeak Bay

bodies and explosive traces consistent with missile impact throughout the wreckage. Radar sightings reported at the time also seemed to suggest a missile. Since then, vital evidence, which was confirmed as recovered at the time, has gone missing from official custody under suspicious circumstances.

The cover-up seems to have proceeded along familiar lines. The CIA report that was used to dismiss the missile theory used faulty evidence and seemed to have been more of a propaganda exercise. The FBI classified many eyewitness statements suggestive of missile impact as "secret," as well as a report on the tests that it commissioned which concluded that a missile was probably to blame. The National Transportation Safety Board (the official investigator) has also withheld evidence. Attempts to get these vital pieces of evidence released have been fought tooth and nail by the FBI and others, although ongoing court cases may produce results.

In 1996, high-profile journalist Pierre Salinger claimed that a source in French intelligence had informed him that the Navy had shot the plane down; he was quickly branded a gullible fool. Investigative journalist Jim Sanders and his wife were taken to court over allegations that they had tampered with the evidence, a gesture typical of the smear tactics used by intelligence agencies to discredit critics

The official line
The initial media noise about the missile theory was based on unsubstantiated "inside" sources that never materialized. A massive four-year investigation by the best experts in the world concluded that the exploding fuel tank explanation was correct.

How paranoid should you be? 45%
The case for a friendly fire disaster followed by a cover-up is compelling and the official investigation was deeply flawed, probably because of FBI interference. At the very least, the relatives of the 230 victims deserve to know the truth.

The Illuminati

An elite secret group intent on fomenting revolution in order to achieve global domination, or mere paranoid fiction?

Several groups throughout history have called themselves the Illuminati, meaning the "Enlightened Ones," but what most people are referring to with the term is the Bavarian Illuminati founded in Ingolstadt, Bavaria, in 1776 by an ex-Jesuit law professor, Adam Weishaupt, and Baron Adolph von Knigge. Its members were drawn almost entirely from the ranks of the Masons. The Bavarian Illuminati was a secret society for freethinkers with Republican ideals that espoused a number of beliefs radical for the time, though fairly unexceptional now. Members included both intellectuals, such as Goethe, and local aristocracy. In the conservative, Catholic, and monarchical Bavaria of the eighteenth century, they were hardly likely to be popular with the authorities and were banned in 1785.

What the theorists say

The stated aim of the Illuminati, as revealed in secret papers written by Weishaupt, was to infiltrate the governments of the world, foment revolution to overthrow existing states and religions, and instigate a single world government. Although officially outlawed, the society lived on in secret, promoting its evil schemes through groups as varied as the Freemasons, the British Royal family, the Bilderbergs, the Trilateral Commission, the Council on Foreign Relations, the European Union, the United Nations, the international Jewish banking conspiracy, the Zionist-Bolshevik conspiracy, Skull and Bones, and many others. Through such influential organizations, the Illuminati grasp the reins of global power and run world affairs like puppet masters, gradually softening up the world's population for the imposition of a new world order. The achievements of the Illuminati so far include the American, French, and Russian Revolutions, the spread of atheism, the creation of the EU, the UN, the World Health Organization, the World Bank, and the International Monetary Fund. Possibly they are in league with aliens to enslave the human race and take over the planet. Possibly they actually *are* aliens!

The official line

Theories about the Illuminati tend to be short on evidence and their quasi-mythical status makes them the perfect candidates for the role of arch villain in the various mega-conspiracy theories. They were first cast in this role in the late eighteenth century when contemporary conspiracy theorists accused them of being mixed up with the Knights Templar and the Freemasons, and of having planned and executed the American and French Revolutions. In reality their membership never exceeded 2,000 and they ceased to exist after 1785, having been riven with internal dissent before this date.

At the very most, they discussed and promoted ideals shared with contemporary revolutionaries, such as the primacy of reason and individual rights over the authority of Church and State. This so terrified the reactionary forces of the establishment that they were roundly demonized.

In the world of modern conspiracies, Illuminati theories owe more to thinly veiled anti-Semitism and feelings of exclusion and alienation from the mainstream.

How paranoid should you be? 0%

Deranged and distasteful anti-Semitic rants about the Illuminati and their new world order simply obscure and detract from genuinely helpful conspiracy research, helping those with something to hide—the secret state, for instance—to dismiss serious researchers as nuts and fruitcakes.

The Protocols of the Elders of Zion

A crude Tsarist hoax plagiarized from fictional sources, which has nonetheless proved to be probably the most dangerous slander in history.

In 1903, a Ukrainian newspaper revealed the existence of an explosive document known as the *Protocols of the Elders of Zion*, the memos of a series of secret meetings by "evil Jews" (the eponymous Elders), in which they outlined their nefarious plan to take over the world. Two years later, a fuller version was published in a book by Sergei Nilus, a Russian mystic.

By 1914, it was a bestseller all over Europe. The existence of the *Protocols* was used to justify the repression of Russian Jews, massive pogroms in which 100,000 Jews were murdered, the assassination of the German foreign minister, and Hitler's Final Solution.

In 1972, a group of Japanese fanatics, enraged by the *Protocols*, killed 24 people at an airport in Israel. Other fans of the *Protocols* have included Henry Ford, Colonel Gaddafi, David Icke, Osama Bin Laden, and the Ku Klux Klan.

What the theorists say

The *Protocols* reveal in chilling detail how the Jews plan to gain control of governments, business, and the media, disrupt economies, undermine moral values and Christianity, bomb cities and infect populations with germ warfare, and eventually assert their dominance over a shattered world. These documents constitute proof that the Jews are orchestrating a global conspiracy against all the peoples of Earth, and have been behind everything from the Great Depression of the 1930s and the two World Wars, to homosexual rights, AIDS, and 9/11.

The official line

Soon after they first "surfaced," the *Protocols* were revealed to be a crude forgery, almost certainly perpetrated by the Okhrana, the Tsarist secret police. The notoriously anti-Semitic chief of the Okhrana, Ivanovich Rachkovsky, is thought to have commissioned the work from one Mathieu Golovinski, a propagandist writer.

Much of the *Protocols* was copied from books on different subjects, with a few words altered here and there. For instance, much of it can be traced directly to Maurice Joly's 1864 political satire *Dialogue in Hell Between Machiavelli and Montesquieu*, in which Napoleon III lays out his evil plot to secure world domination. Golovinski seems to have simply replaced "France" with "Zion" and "Napoleon" with "Jews." Nilus later admitted that Rachkovsky had planned the forgery. Even the anti-Semitic Tsar Nicholas II ordered the *Protocols* be suppressed after realizing they were forged. They have since been exposed by the London *Times* and by numerous writers.

How paranoid should you be? 0%

The sordid tale of the *Protocols* vividly illustrates how conspiracy theories can be used and abused to demonize minorities and support race hatred. Despite their constant unmasking, numerous groups around the world still tout them as proof of a global Jewish conspiracy. The Syrian government still publishes them as a genuine work, while in 2004, the Museum of Manuscripts at the Alexandria Library in Egypt had a copy on display as a real work, describing it as "a holy book for the Jew." This fraud has already contributed to the deaths of millions of Jews; how long must it continue to work its evil?

The Gassers of Tokyo

Could the Aum cult gas attack on the Tokyo subway be just the tip of the iceberg in a complex tale of official corruption and secret Doomsday weapons?

On March 20, 1995, 12 people died and 5,000 people were hospitalized by a sarin nerve gas attack unleashed on Tokyo's underground. Behind the atrocity was the strange and secretive Aum Shinrikyo cult. Soon after, most of its leaders, the perpetrators of the attack, and "Holy Pope" Shoko Asahara, the cult's guru, were in custody and the sect was suppressed (although it survives today in supposedly toothless form under the name "Aleph"). All the senior cult figures are now either dead, in jail, or have served time. Asahara received the death sentence.

What the theorists say

The Tokyo gassing was simply the deadliest in a series of strange goings-on linked to Aum Shinrikyo, a cult that may have gained access to super-secret Doomsday weapons. Aum began as a quasi-Buddhist yoga and health-food cult in the 1980s, but by the 1990s it had become something much darker: a millenarian sect with a belief that Armageddon would shortly arrive, wiping out 90 percent of humanity and leaving only the chosen few. Its sacred task was to bring about this Armageddon, and to this end it pursued the development of biological and chemical weapons of mass destruction. After the subway gassing, investigators found extensive weapons labs stocked with botulinin toxin and smallpox.

Where did Aum obtain the finance and backing for this arsenal of doom? At the time of the arrests, the cult was worth over $1 billion. Much of it came from adherents but there is also strong evidence that the cult had links to the Japanese authorities. It allegedly received extensive funds, for instance, from Shintaro Ishihara, an influential politician and one-time governor of Tokyo, and counted many members of the Japanese military among its sympathizers. Prior to the sarin attacks, the authorities had unaccountably protected the cult from police action, despite several other gas attacks and numerous accusations from escaped cultists.

The cult also had a particularly strong presence in Russia, where there were 30,000 members. It is widely believed the sect was buying top-secret energy-weapons technology from the Russians.

Aum had a strong interest in energy weapons, especially those of the legendary inventor and electricity pioneer Nikolas Tesla. About a century ago, Tesla claimed to have developed a range of terrible energy weapons, including ones that could cause earthquakes using electromagnetic pulses. Much of this research was classified by the US government and remains top secret.

Left Shoko Asahara (born Chizuo Matsumoto), founder of the cult Aum Shinrikyo, as featured in *Time* magazine in July 2002. Central to the beliefs of the cult is the idea that a believer can "remove bad karma" by enduring various sufferings. Members use this idea to justify the abuse of other members.

Incredibly, there is evidence that Aum may have actually acquired some of these weapons.

In 1993, an earthquake was reported in Western Australia—the first ever recorded there. It was linked with sightings of strange beams of light. Investigation showed that the earthquake's epicenter was the Banjawarn sheep station, which had been purchased just weeks earlier by the Aum Shinrikyo cult.

Was the sect testing some sort of energy weapon? Had Aum taken up where the Soviets left off in a secret energy-weapons arms race with the US?

The official line

Tesla was a self-promoting showman who made grand claims to secure funding from gullible backers, and so-called energy weapons are a myth. Cults like Aum have delusions of grandeur, but the relative failure of their subway attack (it was intended to kill thousands) shows how their lofty ambitions were not matched by their technological expertise. Anyway, the cult is now largely disbanded.

How paranoid should you be? 15%

Aum was just one of several powerful cults that seemed to have infiltrated Japanese society at every level and shared in their apocalyptic vision. Indeed, there is evidence that Aum was actually framed over the sarin attack by a rival cult called Soka Gakkai, which has links to the Yakuza, the corrupt politicians governing Japan and the armed forces. Might they be planning other attacks that will make the subway incident look like a tea party?

Part Three:
No One is Safe

The Death of Princess Diana

Was the car crash an accident or was Princess Diana murdered by British secret services at the behest of a vengeful Royal family?

After an acrimonious divorce from Prince Charles in August 1996, relations between Princess Diana and the Royal family had soured. By 1997, she was rumored to be on the verge of announcing her engagement to Dodi Al Fayed, playboy son of Mohammed Al Fayed, owner of Harrods. This was the latest in a string of embarrassments for the Royals, who apparently resented Diana's popularity.

On the night of August 31, 1997, Diana and Dodi, and bodyguard Trevor Rees-Jones, were in a car driven by Henri Paul, the Al Fayeds' security chief, pursued by a pack of paparazzi on motorbikes and in cars (including a white Fiat Uno that was never found). While speeding through an underpass the car, veering to the right as it attempted to pass a slower vehicle on the left, spun out of control and smashed into a pillar. The car was left a mangled mess and the driver and Dodi were killed instantly, leaving Rees-Jones seriously injured, and Diana near death. Rees-Jones survived the accident but, following surgery to restructure his jaw and set a broken arm, he lay in a coma for several weeks and has little memory of anything after the car left the hotel. Diana's injuries were fatal.

What the theorists say

Allegedly, the Royals were horrified by Diana's liaison with Dodi for a number of reasons. Firstly, he was a Muslim and any children they had in the future (the step-siblings of the future king) would be Muslim—which might create an unprecedented scandal. As well as this, Mohammed Al Fayed had been engaged in a long battle with the British establishment over their refusal to grant him a British passport.

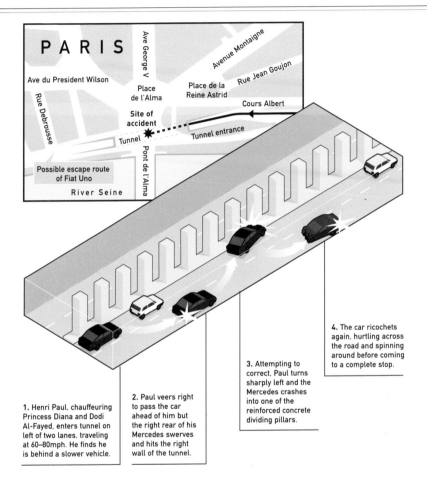

PARIS

Ave du President Wilson

Rue Debrousse

Ave George V

Place de l'Alma

Avenue Montaigne

Rue Jean Goujon

Place de la Reine Astrid

Cours Albert

Site of accident

Tunnel

Pont de l'Alma

Tunnel entrance

Possible escape route of Fiat Uno

River Seine

1. Henri Paul, chauffeuring Princess Diana and Dodi Al-Fayed, enters tunnel on left of two lanes, traveling at 60–80mph. He finds he is behind a slower vehicle.

2. Paul veers right to pass the car ahead of him but the right rear of his Mercedes swerves and hits the right wall of the tunnel.

3. Attempting to correct, Paul turns sharply left and the Mercedes crashes into one of the reinforced concrete dividing pillars.

4. The car ricochets again, hurtling across the road and spinning around before coming to a complete stop.

Seeing his son married to the mother of the future king would have been a remarkable personal triumph for Mohammed Al Fayed, and a corresponding slap in the face for the Royals. "Make no mistake, they were about to become engaged," Mohammed Al Fayed told the *Sunday Times* in June 1997. "I have no doubt that on her return to Britain, the princess would have discussed Dodi's proposal with her sons."

A widely held theory is that Diana was already pregnant when she was killed and that this information is being used by the Royal family to limit the amount of access and influence that Diana's family have to her sons. Even more outlandishly, it has been suggested that Diana was not the target of the "accident" at all. Rather Dodi was the target and it was unfortunate that Diana was in the wrong place at the wrong time.

One of the paparazzi involved, James Andanson, was found dead in mysterious circumstances in May 2000. He owned a white Fiat Uno. Not long after his death, his photo agency, Sipa, was raided by armed, masked men.

Former British intelligence officer Richard Tomlinson suspects that MI6 planned and executed the "accident," causing Paul to crash by blinding him with a strobe flash-gun, in a version of an operation that had been originally planned for the assassination of former Serbian President Slobodan Milosevic. CCTV cameras covering the route were inexplicably turned off.

Paul had received mysterious payments—Tomlinson suggests he was an MI6 informant. It has since come to light that in 1996 Diana recorded on tape her fears that Prince Charles would try to have her murdered . . . in a staged car crash.

The official line

Paul is alleged to have been an alcoholic who was taking prescribed medication. The only witnesses who claim to have seen a bright flash in the tunnel are unreliable or possibly non-existent. Diana was known to be paranoid, so wild accusations against Charles may not be surprising. Extensive French judicial investigations have dismissed any conspiracy theory.

How paranoid should you be? 1%

Al Fayed and others claim the investigations were a farce, that Paul's blood samples were doctored to make it appear he was drunk, and that any accusations of alcoholism were unfounded. However, even suspicious minds have to admit that if it was a plot, it was ill-conceived, for had Diana and Dodi been wearing seatbelts, they would probably have survived.

Death of a Dream

Martin Luther King was not murdered
by a lone assassin but by a CIA/Mafia
conspiracy to remove the most
charismatic black leader of his era.

On April 4, 1968, just a few weeks before a planned march on Washington DC, Martin Luther King was shot in the head by a sniper's bullet as he stood on the balcony of the Lorraine Motel in Memphis, Tennessee. Fingerprints on the murder weapon proved to be those of small-time thief and hustler James Earl Ray, who was arrested in London two months later. After pleading guilty (to avoid the death penalty), he was sentenced to 99 years in jail. Almost immediately afterward he claimed his confession had been bogus, but he died in jail in 1998.

What the theorists say

King was assassinated by a CIA/Mafia hit squad acting on behalf of the military, the FBI, and the white establishment. Ray was framed for the murder in an elaborate operation and subsequent cover-up.

By 1968, King's profile and influence terrified the authorities. The FBI believed he had links to the communists. Army intelligence, which had been watching him for years on account of his vocal opposition to the Vietnam War, feared that his upcoming march on Washington DC was a pretext for a mass riot aimed at shutting down the government.

On the day of his murder, a suspicious number of law enforcement and intelligence agents were in Memphis, yet inexplicably the FBI decided to withdraw its normally constant and intrusive surveillance of King, despite a number of well-known threats on his life. Only two policemen were detailed to guard King and one of them, black officer Detective Ed Reddit, was mysteriously pulled out of position for a meeting with a bevy of police and intelligence chiefs.

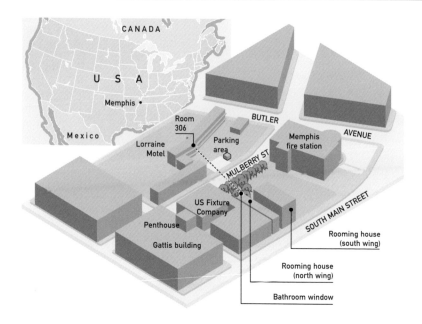

Even more suspect was the evidence relating to Ray, the supposed assassin. A man was seen fleeing the building opposite the Lorraine Motel and conspicuously dropping a bundle on the pavement. This parcel conveniently contained the murder weapon and some of Ray's personal effects, covered in his fingerprints (although his prints were not found in the room where the shot came from or on the box of bullets).

Testimony was given at Ray's trial that not even a crack marksman and a contortionist could have fired and successfully assassinated King from the rooming house opposite. Branches from trees obscured the line of sight from the window to the balcony and it was suggested by the prosecution that Ray, a poor shot in the army, held himself in position around the bathtub to make the shot. Further forensic tests on the evidence in question in 1997 conclusively proved the bullet that killed King did not come from the weapon with which the authorities maintain the murder was committed.

Despite this evidence that Ray was not the assassin, the prosecution maintain that he somehow eluded capture and made it to Toronto, where a mysterious "fat man" gave him a bundle of cash that he used to flee to Europe en route to Angola.

Prior to the assassination, Ray had employed a series of Canadian aliases despite never having been there. Ray himself claimed he was forced into the false confession by his Mafia-linked lawyer and that he was set up as the patsy by a man named "Raoul," who he thought was an arms dealer. Subsequent investigation has suggested that a CIA agent named Raoul Miora was on assignment in Canada around that time. His speciality? Fake identities.

In short, small-time crook Ray was recruited by the CIA, shuttled around America until arriving in Memphis, where he was told to buy a rifle, and put up in a boarding room. A Ray lookalike committed the murder and dropped the damning evidence in full view of the public. Ray was then helped to escape and later forced to take the rap.

The official line

Naturally Ray tried to weasel out of his guilt once convicted, but his story is patently absurd. In 2000, Attorney General Janet Reno opened a probe into the case, which concluded there was no credible evidence to back up the conspiracy claim.

How paranoid should you be? 75%

The evidence points to a frame-up—it seems Ray could not have been King's killer. Vital documents relating to the case remain classified, so expect to wait another 60 years to learn the truth.

Candle in the Wind

Marilyn Monroe's death was not a simple case of suicide. She was murdered to protect or possibly blackmail the Kennedy brothers.

On August 4, 1962, screen siren Marilyn Monroe was found dead in the bedroom of her home in Brentwood, California. She was 36 years old. Officially she died of a drug overdose. However, no residues were found in her stomach. It is widely believed that an ambulance was actually called five hours before the official alert only to turn back and return her to her home.

What the theorists say

Monroe was both Jack (John) and Bobby (Robert) Kennedy's lover. As a result, her residence was bugged by both the FBI and the Mob. She had been introduced to the Kennedys by Peter Lawford, a Rat Pack member with Mob links, and by Mob boss Sam Giancana, who may also have had an affair with the actress and wanted to keep tabs on her liaisons, possibly for blackmail purposes. J. Edgar Hoover, head of the FBI, had similar motives. He hated and feared the Kennedy brothers because they had threatened his position and he wanted to compile evidence against them to protect himself.

Meanwhile, the two brothers had got themselves dangerously tangled up with Monroe. The story is that Jack simply viewed her as a diversion and cast her lightly aside, at which point Monroe started to kick up a fuss, risking exposure that would be fatal to the President's position. Bobby began a relationship with her to divert Marilyn from Jack, but then fell in love with her. As Monroe's behavior became increasingly erratic, with mood swings and heavy drug use, she became a liability for them both. In August 1962, after she made hysterical threats over the phone, something had to give.

There are three main versions of what happened next. The first theory is that Bobby Kennedy, worried about Monroe after her alarming phone call, came round to discover that she had accidentally taken an overdose. He called an ambulance, but on the way to the hospital, realized she was already dead. To avoid a scandal, he had the body put back in the bed while he made his escape. The second theory is that possibly the Mob or government agents murdered Monroe to get the Kennedys off the hook. The third theory is that either the FBI or the Mob killed Marilyn so they could, if necessary, link her death back to the Kennedys and thus blackmail them. These murder theories explain why no drug residue was found in her stomach as the fatal dose had been administered by suppository. This accounts for an odd remark Lawford is said to have made about Monroe's death at the time: "Marilyn took her last big enema." Supposedly the extensive bugging of Monroe's household yielded tapes that back up one or other of these theories and numerous people claim to have heard them.

The official line
The doctor who performed the autopsy on Monroe said that her death was probably a suicide and she was well known to have been depressed and erratic in previous months. She was also reckless in her use of uppers and downers, and perhaps misjudged a dose of the latter. A 1982 investigation by the LA District Attorney concluded that there was no credible evidence of foul play.

How paranoid should you be? 3%
The "unofficial" ambulance ride can be explained by the unwillingness of the hospital St John's in Santa Monica to deal with the scandal that such a celebrity admission would have caused. Perhaps the most obvious flaw in the "she was killed to protect JFK" theory is that his many other mistresses, who included the far more potentially embarrassing Judith Campbell Exner, a known moll of Sam Giancana, outlived him. As for the alleged tapes, if they were made, where are they? A figure like Monroe inevitably inspired salacious stories about her death but this does not mean they are true.

The Lone Gunman

Lee Harvey Oswald was not acting in isolation but may have been working for the FBI, the CIA, the anti-Castro Cubans, or even the Russian KGB.

On November 22, 1963, President John F. Kennedy was assassinated in Dallas, Texas. Lee Harvey Oswald was arrested for the crime after being matched to witness sightings of a man pointing a rifle out of a window at the Texas Book Store Depository, from where a rifle bearing his prints was later recovered, after he gunned down a police officer who tried to question him. Two days later, he was shot dead by a Mafia hoodlum and sometime FBI informant Jack Ruby. The Warren Commission, set up to look into the killings, concluded that Oswald was the sole assassin.

What the theorists say

Almost as soon as he was picked up, the authorities painted Oswald as an archetypal lone nut: the perfect culprit for an open-and-shut case that would satisfy the public without raising embarrassing questions. What the establishment was afraid of was the mass of leads that suggested Oswald actually might have been working for anyone from the KGB to the FBI. Some of these leads are detailed below.

Oswald had supposedly been a communist since the age of 15; however, he joined the Marines as a young man. Despite being openly communist, the Marines posted him to Atsugi, in Japan, the base for ultra top-secret U2 spy plane operations. He was taught Russian (something very unusual for a common grunt). In 1959, he was discharged and defected to the Soviet Union, apparently because of his political principles. However, a declassified CIA memo says Oswald was a CIA recruit given special indoctrination and deliberately sent to Russia. This explains how he got the money for the ticket to Russia in the first place.

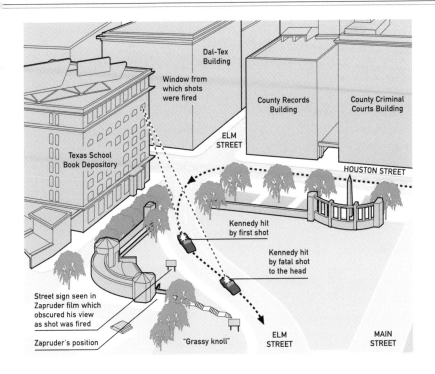

Dal-Tex
Building

Window from
which shots
were fired

County Records
Building

County Criminal
Courts Building

ELM
STREET

HOUSTON STREET

Texas School
Book Depository

Kennedy hit
by first shot

Kennedy hit
by fatal shot
to the head

Street sign seen in
Zapruder film which
obscured his view
as shot was fired

Zapruder's position

"Grassy knoll"

ELM
STREET

MAIN
STREET

In 1962, Oswald, now married, was allowed to move back to the US with remarkably little fuss. In April 1963, he moved to New Orleans and became involved with a very suspicious trio of right-wing, anti-Castro activists: Guy Bannister, a former FBI agent; Clay Shaw, a suspected CIA agent; and David Ferrie, an amateur pilot with strong anti-Castro and CIA links. Oswald and Ferrie had been in the same Civil Air Guard unit when the former was just 15. Oswald also befriended a group of anti-Castro Cubans, despite apparently being a pro-Castro activist. They were soon involved in a "staged" street fight.

Around August 1963, Oswald supposedly went to Mexico City to visit the Cuban Embassy, although the description given by a CIA agent who kept tabs on him there patently describes a different man. At around the same time, Oswald was seen in Dallas in the company of a man later identified as right-wing CIA officer David Atlee Phillips.

When Oswald's body was buried, it was said to be missing vital scars; in other words, it wasn't him! Some writers speculate that while Oswald was in Russia, the KGB had him switched for a lookalike who was actually a trained assassin. Senior members of the Warren Commission, on the other hand, speculated that Oswald had been an FBI informant and that they seemed overly keen to close his file.

As well as this mountain of information about Oswald's ties to various organizations, the hard forensic evidence also seems to suggest that Oswald could not have acted alone. Many experts insist that four shots were fired, but only three have ever been accounted for and it has not been adequately proven that they all came from the same direction. The President was hit by two bullets, one in the back and one in the head. Another passenger in the vehicle, Texan Governor John B. Connally, was hit, along with bystander James T. Tague. The Warren Commision concluded that one of the bullets struck Tague, another bullet struck Kennedy in the head, and the third bullet, known as the "magic" bullet, struck both Connally and Kennedy. This bullet was somehow responsible for seven wounds to two men, though this doesn't seem to tally with its timing, flight path, the points of entry and exit, and the resulting condition of the bullet. Further forensic proof was offered in 1979 to attempt to prove that it was a single bullet that wounded both Kennedy and Connally; however, for every forensic scientist skeptical of multiple-bullet theories, there seems to be at least one opposite and equal scientist supportive of them.

In summary, it is not clear who Oswald was working with, but there is a mass of evidence to show he was not working alone.

The official line

Most of what conspiracy theorists say about Oswald is either unsupported or just plain inaccurate. Almost all of the previous "evidence" can be explained or rebutted. Oswald was posted to the U2 base but so were thousands of other soldiers; he had nothing to do with the U2 activities and was mostly confined to menial duties; the man did not learn Russian from the Marines but was self-taught. Records show he planned his defection carefully, saving his pay to afford the ticket. The CIA memo claiming him as an agent is probably a forgery. The US did not welcome him back with open arms; it took him a year of patient waiting and red tape to regain his citizenship.

Oswald probably befriended the anti-Castro Cubans in New Orleans in a clumsy attempt to infiltrate the group. The street scuffle happened when they realized he was pro-Cuban and it was never described as "staged," as has been alleged. There is no proof he knew Bannister, Shaw, or Ferrie in New Orleans, and no evidence that he and Ferrie knew each other while serving in the same Civil Air Guard unit.

His trip to Mexico City was an attempt to get a visa to go to Cuba. Claims that Oswald was seen elsewhere at this time are probably simple mistakes made in the excitement that followed his arrest and death. Dozens of spurious sightings were reported. The link to Phillips has been convincingly disproved. As for the assassination itself, we know that Oswald was capable of it because in April he had tried to kill a prominent anti-Communist, retired General Edwin Walker (with the same rifle that was later used to shoot JFK). When Oswald's body was exhumed to test the KGB switch theory, dental records confirmed his identity.

How paranoid should you be? 44%

It does seem that almost every suspicious fact about Oswald can be explained or simply helps to build up a picture of someone who may very well have tried to assassinate the president. However, the Oswald facts are just fragments in the vast mosaic of evidence that JFK was killed by a conspiracy and not by a lone gunman.

Whitewater Blowback

Bill Clinton's attorney Vince Foster did not commit suicide but was murdered to cover up a presidential scandal.

On July 20, 1993, the body of Vince Foster, Deputy Counsel to the White House and personal friend and lawyer of Bill and Hillary Clinton, was discovered slumped beneath a tree in Fort Marcy Park, Virginia. The coroner ruled that he had committed suicide by putting a revolver in his mouth and pulling the trigger.

What the theorists say

Many aspects of Foster's life and death do not add up. For instance, his body was officially found in Fort Marcy Park after an anonymous 911 call, but the initial Secret Service report says that Foster was found in his car, and a state trooper in Arkansas claims to have heard about the suicide from a White House aide several hours before the White House officially knew of the death. Foster had spent the morning of his death working busily in his office, just like any other day. Despite being equipped with the most sophisticated entry control system and video surveillance in the world, no record exists showing Foster leaving the White House on July 20, 1993, however. The autopsy seems to have been bungled; many people claim that photos of the body showed no exit wound at the back of the head or entry wounds in the neck. There was little blood at the scene, no bullet fragments were recovered, and Foster's fingerprints were not identified on the gun, which suggest that the body was moved there after death. Expert analysis of a suicide note that was found in Foster's briefcase has concluded that it was forged.

What really happened? Conspiracy theorists argue that Foster was murdered because he knew far too much about two scandals threatening the

Clinton presidency, which only emerged after his death. The Whitewater Affair, where the Clintons were accused of fraud in relation to a real estate company that went bust, and the Health Management Associates (HMA) scandal, where a company run by a close Clinton friend, supporter, and fundraiser was said to have sold tainted blood to Canada. As the Clinton's friend and lawyer, Foster is alleged to have known more than was healthy about the scandals, or possibly to have been overcome with guilt. Adding to the mystery is the revelation that Foster had flown regularly to Switzerland on tickets bought with an "executive fare" discount before he was officially a member of any administration (and therefore before he was eligible for such perks). Was Foster a government agent?

The official line

Vince Foster was a principled idealist who struggled to cope with the backbiting cruelty of Washington. His senior position in the White House did not sit well with him. Days after a public speech stressing the value of personal integrity, he had confided to family and friends that he was considering resigning from his position. He had even written an outline for a resignation letter. He had been the victim of personal attacks in prominent newspapers and his friendship with Hillary had cooled. He had recently asked his doctor to prescribe him anti-depressants.

Foster's suicide note mentioned the newspaper attacks and complained that in Washington "ruining people is considered a sport." Independent Counsel Robert Fiske investigated the incident and concluded it was suicide. Other independent inquiries exonerated the Clintons; in other words, there was nothing to cover up. The conspiracy theories are the work of Republicans desperate to discredit Clinton.

How paranoid should you be? 5%

Though questions remain, it seems likely that Foster did indeed commit suicide and was a casualty of Washington life. Perhaps tasteless Republican conspiracy theories are simply the final indignity for Foster. Of course, that's what the Democrats will tell you . . .

RFK and the Brainwashed Assassin

The CIA brainwashed and programed Sirhan Sirhan to attempt to kill Robert F. Kennedy but the real assassin was a CIA agent.

On June 5, 1968, Robert Kennedy (RFK) was accosted at the Ambassador Hotel in Los Angeles by Sirhan Sirhan, a crazed gunman who emptied a pistol at him. RFK subsequently died and Sirhan was convicted and sentenced to death, although a change in Californian law spared his life at the eleventh hour.

What the theorists say

At the time of his death, RFK was about to secure the Democratic nomination for presidential candidate and would surely have won. The same forces that had conspired to murder his brother were even more fearful now; Kennedy had to die. His assassination is one of the most clear-cut cases of conspiracy and cover-up in American history.

Sirhan Sirhan was brainwashed and hypnotically programed by CIA elements using techniques developed in the MK-ULTRA program (see pages 135–136). His job was to act as a decoy, drawing attention away from the real shooter. We know this because ballistics proved that all the shots fired by Sirhan missed Kennedy and hit the walls, ceiling, or bystanders instead. Sirhan cannot remember anything about the event and witnesses report that he appeared to be in a trance. He also proved to be remarkably susceptible to hypnosis. A hypnosis expert who worked on the MK-ULTRA program allegedly boasted of having worked on Sirhan.

Several more bullet holes than can be accounted for from Sirhan's weapon were found lodged in the walls and ceiling, while the autopsy evidence very clearly showed that RFK was shot from behind at point-blank range.

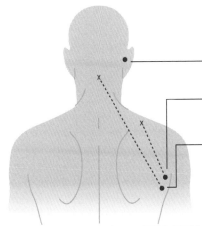

Fatal shot entered through the mastoid bone, 1 inch behind the right ear, and traveled upward to sever the branches of the superior cerebral artery. The largest fragment of that bullet lodged in the brain stem.

Another shot penetrated the right armpit and exited through the upper portion of the chest at a 59-degree angle.

A third shot entered 1.5 inches below the previous one and stopped in the neck near the sixth cervical. This bullet was found intact.

Kennedy's clothing indicated that a fourth bullet had been fired at the senator. It entered and exited the fabric without touching his body.

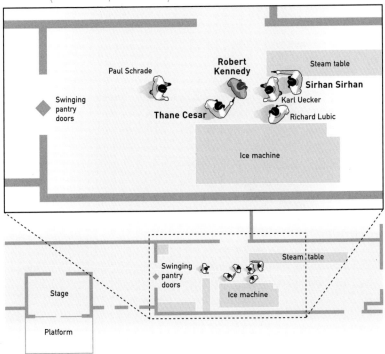

Paul Schrade

Robert Kennedy

Steam table

Sirhan Sirhan

Karl Uecker

Thane Cesar

Richard Lubic

Swinging pantry doors

Ice machine

Steam table

Swinging pantry doors

Stage

Ice machine

Platform

Witnesses all agree that Sirhan was in front of RFK at least three feet away. The most likely killer was Thane Cesar, a security guard believed to have CIA links. He was seen to pull his gun and fire, and was exactly where the autopsy evidence suggested the shooter must have been.

The LAPD engaged in a poorly concealed cover-up, intimidating witnesses, failing to follow up leads, and destroying evidence, including burning all the photos of the murder scene, but even their own ballistics expert initially reported findings inconsistent with Sirhan as the shooter. Several witnesses reported seeing a girl in a polka-dot dress fleeing the scene shouting, "We shot him, we shot him!" The same person had earlier been seen talking to Sirhan. Police bullied the witnesses into changing their testimonies. The LAPD cops in charge of the investigation supposedly had ties to the CIA.

The official line

A thorough investigation concluded that Sirhan was the sole killer, a Palestinian who wanted revenge for Kennedy's support of Israel. Sirhan may well have been in a trance but it was, as one of the psychiatrists examining him concluded, a self-induced trance. Claims about extra bullet holes are not backed up by evidence at the scene and confusion over the ballistics tests was down to clerical errors. Cesar only drew his pistol in response to Sirhan's shots and never actually fired it. He later passed a lie detector test on his role in the shooting. There is no proof that he had any involvement with the CIA.

How paranoid should you be? 29%

If the LAPD investigation into the RFK shooting is genuine, it must rank as one of the worst investigations of all time. So was it a cover-up? The manner of the shooting fits in with CIA hit tactics: one shooter distracts attention while another does the job. In this case, perhaps the decoy was also the patsy. If Californian law had not changed at the last minute, Sirhan would have been conveniently disposed of, like Lee Harvey Oswald. To date, Sirhan has been refused parole 12 times. On the other hand, most psychologists doubt that it would genuinely be possible to "program" someone to kill and also to forget everything about the programming process.

P2 and the Death of the Pope

The death of Pope John Paul I in 1978 was more than an unfortunate tragedy. He was murdered by an alliance of Mafiosi, crooked clergy, and P2.

Albino Luciani was elected Pope on August 26, 1978, and he subsequently chose the name John Paul I. Thirty-three days later, he was dead, officially from a heart attack.

What the theorists say

John Paul I was murdered to prevent him from blowing the whistle on dirty dealing at the Vatican Bank and on the malign influence inside the Church of a Masonic secret society called P2. This was a Masonic Lodge that had been created by Italian Fascist Licio Gelli in the 1960s. Under Italian law, membership of the Freemasons had to be registered and Roman Catholic clergy were forbidden to join. Gelli set up P2 as a secret lodge, where only he knew the full membership. He recruited followers from the ranks of the powerful and influential sectors of Catholic society, including the Mafia, the Church, the secret services, the military, government, business, and finance. P2 helped to create links between crooks, dictators, and financiers in Italy, Spain, and Latin America; more specifically, it helped to involve the Vatican Bank in money laundering on a massive scale.

When John Paul I became Pope, he soon realized that the Vatican Bank was up to no good and a list sent to him by a journalist who was later murdered revealed that many of the highest-ranking clergy in the Church were also P2 members. Before the Pope could blow the whistle, he was poisoned. Declared dead from a heart attack, his body was quickly embalmed before an autopsy could be performed, and his organs were disposed of.

The papers he was reading on the night of his death went missing. His successor, Pope John Paul II, was a staunch anti-communist who was happy to protect the right-wing alliance that had murdered his predecessor.

The official line

John Paul I's death was tragic but not suspicious and his portrayal as a brilliant sleuth penetrating the moral maze of Vatican finance and politics is a false one. In all honesty, John Paul I was not up to the demands of his job, frequently complaining to anyone who would listen that he should not have been chosen, and proving to have a feeble grasp of the complex business network of the Church. The Pope also suffered from very poor health and Vatican healthcare was unanimously acknowledged as a disgrace. John Paul I suffered from severe heart problems and, on the eve of his death, showed all the signs of an incipient heart attack but refused medical care. He was probably embalmed in a hurry because of the hot weather. When the previous Pope had died, there had been an embarrassing incident where the body had lain in state, rotting to the extent that the nose had fallen off! Vatican officials were desperate to avoid a repeat. The supposedly stolen documents turned up in the possession of John Paul I's family and proved to be nothing sinister. The suggestion that a modern-day pope would have colluded in the cover-up of a murder is offensive.

How paranoid should you be? 12%

The evidence of Pope John Paul I's poor health is incontrovertible so it is not necessary to go looking for a conspiracy that would explain his sudden death after only a very short term in office. However, there is little doubt that his death did benefit certain factions of the Church. In immediate terms, many of the people involved in the P2/Vatican Bank scandal were protected from investigation and censure by the new Pope. In broader terms, John Paul I had been preparing radical changes to the structure of the Church, as well as making controversial moves to soften the official line on birth control. With his death, conservative factions of the Church gained the upper hand for decades to come.

Elvis Lives!

The King faked his own death to escape the pressures of fame, the shame of decline, and even the unwanted attentions of the Mob.

Elvis Aron Presley died on August 16, 1977 and was buried the very next day in an open-coffin funeral.

What the theorists say

There are a number of strange discrepancies surrounding the death and burial of Elvis. The actual cause of death was never properly ascertained but is generally blamed on a lethal cocktail of drugs. In actuality, Elvis was an expert self-doser, knew exactly what he was taking, and it is highly unlikely he would have accidentally overdosed.

When he was buried, his coffin was huge, heavy, and obviously specially made, yet the funeral was almost immediate. Why was it held so quickly? To prevent people who might have recognized him from making it to the burial? Witnesses report that the air around the coffin was unnaturally cool. Was it so heavy because it contained an air-conditioning unit used to refrigerate a wax double of Elvis's body? This theory would help to explain why photos of the body showed it looked quite different from that of the real Elvis, with a pug nose and soft hands (the King's hands were calloused from karate). If the artist really did fake his death, this bizarre twist would make sense of why his family was happy to let his name remain misspelled on his gravestone (his middle name "Aron" should have had only one "a"), an oversight which his father would never otherwise have allowed. The death certificate incorrectly lists his final weight at 170 pounds (77 kilograms), some 80 pounds (36 kilograms) lighter than his last-known weight. This is not the original certificate, however, and is actually dated two months following his death. Interestingly, his life insurance policy was never cashed in.

So why would Elvis want to fake his own demise? It is well known that he was weary of the constant pressure of fame and felt trapped by his own celebrity status, which made leading a normal life impossible. It has also been suggested that he was in danger from a Mob outfit called The Fraternity over a business deal gone wrong and that he went into the witness protection program to help the government bring them down.

The official line

During his last weeks of life, Elvis fell increasingly prey to food and drug binges; it was inevitable that something had to give. His family and everyone closest to him confirm that he did indeed die, and plenty of people who knew Elvis well can testify to having seen his real body in the coffin.

How paranoid should you be? 1%

It is easy to dismiss Elvis conspiracy theories as supermarket tabloid junk or the ravings of loonies but we know that the King did try to fake his death at least once in a bizarre incident involving a bogus assassin and fake blood. He certainly had reason enough to try again. Who is to say he is not out there, preparing for that final comeback tour?

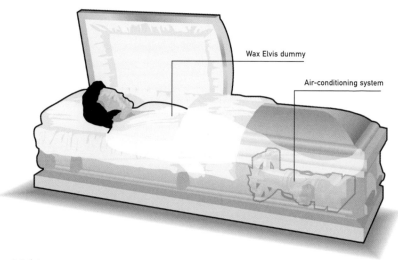

Wax Elvis dummy

Air-conditioning system

Gone Fishin'?

Australian Prime Minister Harold Holt mysteriously disappeared off a beach in 1967. Was it a drowning, suicide, CIA or Chinese conspiracy?

On December 17, 1967, Australian Prime Minister Harold Holt was on Cheviot Beach at Point Nepean, Victoria, holidaying with friends. Apparently seeking to impress his companions, the 59-year-old plunged into the surf and was never seen again. No traces of his body or clothes were ever recovered and he was declared dead on December 19.

What the theorists say

Holt's supposed death by drowning is highly suspicious. He was a strong swimmer well known for his love of skin diving, spear fishing, and watersports in general. In the aftermath of his disappearance, the government insisted that only one person, a government official, had been present with Holt on the beach, but it later transpired he had been with an alleged lover and some other young women. If the government was willing to cover this up, what else were they not telling?

There are four main theories about Holt's death. Firstly, it is claimed that Holt committed suicide, depressed by the recent death of his brother and growing criticism about his leadership.

Another theory, based on "inside sources from the security services," is that he faked his own death by simply swimming around to the next bay, where he was met by a lover and jetted off to the south of France to live out his days.

Thirdly, it has even been suggested he was murdered by the CIA. Holt had been a strong supporter of American involvement in Vietnam but the suggestion is that, faced with growing domestic unpopularity on this stance, he was effectively preparing to pull out Australian forces from Southeast Asia.

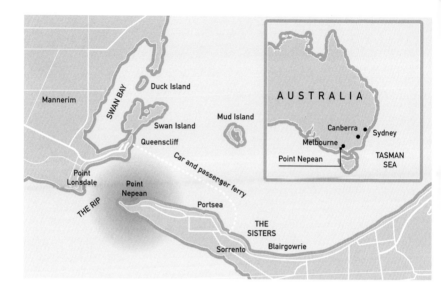

Above Australian Prime Minister Harold Holt disappeared in the surf off Point Nepean beach, in Victoria, on December 17, 1967. Did he commit suicide? Did he simply swim around to the next bay in order to stage his own death? Or did the CIA murder him?

He was finished off by the CIA to make room for someone with more amenable views. His successor, John Gorton, did indeed escalate Australian involvement in Vietnam.

Lastly, some theorists point to British journalist Anthony Grey's claim that Holt had been a Chinese spy all along; on that fateful day, he swam out to a waiting Chinese submarine and was "collected," his assignment now complete.

The official line

Holt had been a strong swimmer for most of his life, but by the time of his death, he was 59 years of age, and was still getting over a recent shoulder injury. The police officer in charge of the investigation into his disappearance said that he thought the Prime Minister "believed he couldn't drown . . . He got into trouble [in the water] and couldn't get himself out." A joint report by Commonwealth and Victoria Police, submitted in January 1968, concluded that, " . . . there has been no indication that the disappearance of the late Mr Holt was anything other than accidental." The report found that his last movements followed a routine domestic pattern, his demeanour had been normal and, despite his knowledge of the beach, the turbulent conditions (high winds, rough seas, and riptides) overcame him. The explanations put forward for a failure to find the body included an attack by marine life, the body being carried out to sea by tides, or the body becoming wedged in rock crevices. Australia's beaches are infamous for such conditions.

The Commonwealth government of Australia, despite the theories, did not consider a formal inquiry necessary and accepted the findings and conclusions of the police report. Claims about the CIA or the Chinese are simply kooky nonsense. Holt was a supporter of involvement in Vietnam, while in 1967, the Chinese Navy did not possess a submarine capable of traveling to Australia and back. As far as suicide goes, there is no evidence he was depressed.

How paranoid should you be? 1%

If a high-profile figure disappears, and no trace of a body is ever found, talk is inevitable. However, there is not a shred of evidence that Holt's death was anything but a simple tragedy.

Princess Grace and the Solar Temple

Princess Grace of Monaco's death in a car accident in 1982 was linked to her membership of a sinister cult that claimed the lives of over 100 people.

On September 13, 1982, Princess Grace of Monaco (formerly film star Grace Kelly) was involved in a car accident and died the next day. The official explanation was that she had suffered a stroke while driving.

What the theorists say

Princess Grace's death was no accident, but was linked in some way to her involvement with a sinister cult known as the Order of the Solar Temple. The Solar Temple, as it is usually known, is a francophone cult that claims to have descended from the Knights Templar. Its founders, con men Joseph di Mambro and Luc Jouret, used hypnosis, stage magic, illusion, and brainwashing to defraud, rape, and eventually murder initiates drawn from the wealthy elite of France, Monaco, Quebec, and Switzerland.

In 1994, members of the cult, believing that they would ascend to the star Sirius as purified beings, committed mass suicide at locations in Quebec and Switzerland. Several people, including children, evidently unwilling to leave the planet, were murdered.

Back in 1982, di Mambro was in the south of France, looking for rich recruits and finding several among the socialites of the Cote d'Azur. One of these was Jean-Louis Marsan, personal friend of Prince Rainier, and he in turn introduced Princess Grace to the cult.

Grace was frustrated and bored by life in Monaco, and longed for excitement and sensuality. The Solar Temple provided these, with exotic rituals that used holograms and stage magic to convince participants that they were witnessing the materialisation of the Holy Grail and the Ark of the Covenant, and that di Mambro and Jouret had occult powers. Grace was initiated by having sex with Jouret during a magical ceremony, and proceeded to give the Order millions of dollars. When she became disillusioned with the Order and threatened to reclaim her funds, di Mambro and Jouret murdered her by causing the crash. Alternatively, she committed suicide in a bizarre display of loyalty to the Order—perhaps they had convinced her that she would ascend to a higher spiritual plane.

The official line

There is no evidence to link Princess Grace to di Mambro, Jouret, or even the Solar Temple. The main source for the lurid tale was a man called Guy Mouyrin, a convicted con man whose claim to have been di Mambro's driver at the time is completely unsubstantiated. The Order of the Solar Temple did not exist until 1984, although in 1982 di Mambro and Jouret were involved in a similar cult that later gave rise to the Solar Temple.

How paranoid should you be? 2%

This story seems to owe little to the truth and more to shoddy journalism and the sensationalist lies of a con man. The Solar Temple, on the other hand, were all too real, and police in Quebec, France, and Switzerland continue to keep a close watch on surviving members who may well attempt further mass suicides.

Part Four:
Sci-fi
Conspiracies

Nazi UFOs

Super-advanced saucer technology
secretly developed by Nazi scientists
was stolen by the US to create a
UFO fleet.

In the closing stages of World War II an increasingly deluded Hitler accelerated his advanced technology Vengeance Weapon programs, which he believed would turn the tide for the Nazis. Though some of these programs bore fruit with the V1 and V2 rockets and early jet fighters, most historians agree that they diverted resources that could have been used more effectively elsewhere, and did not have any real impact on the course of the war. Allied and Russian forces scrambled to get their hands on the Nazis' technological "loot"—most famously in America's Operation Paperclip, where Werner von Braun, his team of rocket scientists, and much of their hardware, were spirited away to the US to form the basis of the American missile and space rocket program.

What the theorists say

A number of Nazi scientists worked on flying disc technology, most notably Austrian energy technology pioneer Viktor Schauberger. Schauberger was personally recruited into the SS by Hitler and sent to work at the Mauthausen concentration camp, where he used slave labour to research and construct prototype flying discs. (According to some versions, Schauberger was a pacifist who objected but was threatened with death if he did not co-operate.) He had immediate success with a machine so powerful that it tore out its anchor bolts and shot through the roof of the hangar. Further research by Schauberger and others led to the development of a range of flying "hats," "disks," and others. In one test, in February 1945, a flying disk achieved an altitude of 50,000 feet (15,000 meters) and a speed of 1,370 miles per hour (2,200 kilometers per hour). Only the invasion of the Axis heartlands put a stop to the program.

After the war, Schauberger was taken to work in Texas, where technology stolen from him and others was used as the basis for a fleet of US flying saucers. These gave rise to the waves of UFO sightings that began in 1947. To provide cover for their top-secret program, the authorities were happy to help spread implausible suggestions that UFOs were alien spaceships. Schauberger was later beaten to death, possibly by organized criminals seeking his secrets.

The official line

Tales of Nazi UFOs are entirely fictional. There is no genuine physical or photographic evidence for any of the claims made by Nazi UFO authors, who often prove to have unsavory agendas, such as pro-Nazi propaganda and Holocaust denial. Schauberger was a hydroelectric engineer who unsuccessfully attempted to develop turbine technology. Some of his designs were vaguely disk-shaped, and photos of these have been touched up to include Luftwaffe insignia and passed off as flying saucers. There is no evidence that Schauberger ever met Hitler, was recruited by the SS, went to Mauthausen, or had anything to do with flight technology. He did visit the US after the war, but soon returned home to Austria where he died peacefully.

How paranoid should you be? 0%

The Nazi UFO mythology is a good example of the way in which baseless theories can become part of "folk wisdom" in the conspiracy field. There are many books about Nazi UFOs, but each new one tends simply to repeat the fictions of earlier ones, embroidering the story a little each time. The Schauberger fiction, for instance, can be traced back to an author called Ernst Zundel, who later admitted that his sensationalist books were a tool for spreading revisionist history about the Holocaust and anti-Semitic propaganda: "the money I made from the UFO books I invested in publishing the booklets *The Auschwitz Lie . . . A Straight Look at the Third Reich . . .* and *Did Six Million Really Die?*" In other words, propagating lies about Nazi UFOs is not simply harmless fun.

Moon Shot Shinola

NASA faked the first moon landings in a publicity coup and produced the world-famous photos and video footage in a Nevada studio.

On July 21, 1969, Neil Armstrong set foot on the lunar surface, watched by a worldwide television audience of millions. Over the next three years, there were five more successful landings and NASA released hundreds of photographs taken by the astronauts. Not long after came the first suggestions that the whole thing had been an elaborate hoax, and even today, some surveys indicate that around 10 percent of the US population believe such a theory, while Cuban children are actually taught it in school. In 2002, NASA decided to commission respected space writer James Oberg to pen a definitive rebuttal to the rumors but changed their minds a few months later.

What the theorists say

The US was desperate to prove its technological prowess to the world while NASA was anxious to secure continued federal funding, but the ambitious plan to land on the Moon proved to be an impossible mission, partly because of the high radiation levels in outer space, which would have proven fatal to the astronauts. It was decided to fake the landings in a studio; the actual rocket re-entered the atmosphere soon after the launch and was ditched into the ocean. The evidence for this is overwhelming, largely thanks to the efforts of whistleblowers among the studio technicians who ensured the photos were riddled with errors as clues.

The main flaw with the so-called "lunar surface photographs" is the lighting. There should only be one light source, the Sun, on the surface of the Moon, and in conjunction with the atmospheric vacuum, this should produce a very strong contrast between lit areas and shadows. Yet the photographs clearly show elements that should be in shadow as often lit with "fill-in"

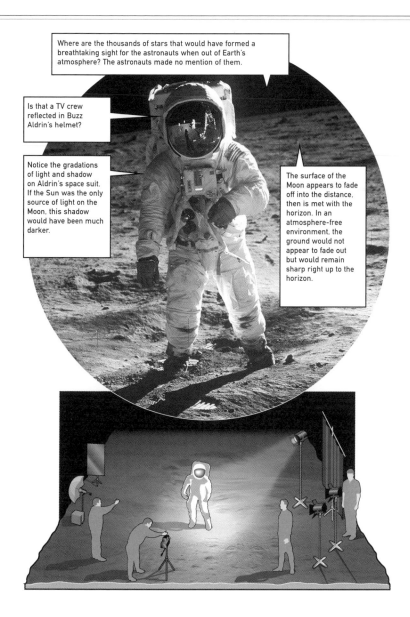

lighting and reflections are thrown from multiple light sources. Furthermore, the shadows cast by different objects in the same shot run at different angles and the ground beneath the landing module shows no evidence of a blast crater. No stars are visible anywhere. Shooting decent photography on the Moon would have proven impossible anyway given the equipment that was available then: an unshielded camera with no viewfinder which had to be operated while wearing thick, immobile gloves. Any film would have been ruined by the high temperatures on the lunar surface and the heavy radiation would have been deadly to the astronauts. NASA's strange behavior with regards to Oberg's book is proof that they have something to hide.

The official line

These criticisms display a total ignorance of atmospheric conditions on the Moon. Many of its surfaces are highly reflective as the Earth provides a source of light in addition to the Sun. (The full Earth seen from the Moon is 68 times brighter than a full Moon on Earth.) Shadows appear to fall at different angles because of the unevenness on the Moon's surface. There was no crater because NASA chose a very solid spot to touch down on. Numerous experiments had demonstrated that the risk from radiation was not as great as feared. The astronauts were highly trained in operating cameras that had been adapted for use with gloves.

By relying on photographic evidence alone, one ignores the mass of irrefutable proof there was a visit, such as the laser reflectors left on the Moon's surface which are still used for recording lunar quakes today. Oberg's book was cancelled because NASA got rattled by media critics who said it was a waste of money pandering to crackpots. Suggestions of a fraud are insulting to the highly dedicated team that worked on the missions, especially the brave astronauts.

How paranoid should you be? 0%

These fake moon landings seem to be another one of those conspiracies that would simply be impossible to cover up, not least because Soviet intelligence would have sniffed out a hoax. It is time to put this old wives' tale to bed.

Roswell

A UFO crashed in New Mexico in 1947 and technology and alien bodies were recovered. The US military has been trying to cover this up ever since.

On July 8, 1947, the *Roswell Daily Record*, local newspaper of the town of Roswell, New Mexico, carried the extraordinary headline "Roswell Army Air Field Captures Flying Saucer on Ranch in Roswell Region." Earlier that week, a local rancher had discovered a field of debris composed of materials he did not recognize and alerted the authorities. The military soon arrived to remove the wreckage to Roswell Army Air Field for analysis. Later it was taken to Wright Field in Ohio. Based on a military press release which referred to a "flying disk, hexagonal in shape," the story was picked up and caused a sensation around the world. Later that afternoon, the Air Force issued a statement to indicate that the wreckage was simply a crashed weather balloon.

What the theorists say

Research by ufologists uncovered numerous witness statements that contradicted the official line. Ranchers and Air Force personnel who had seen the wreckage insisted it was made of metals unknown to science, while a woman who had worked for the military in the region spoke of bodies recovered from the wreckage. A nurse at the Roswell base hospital gave details of the bodies, which were obviously not human. In 1994, a film of an autopsy on the alien corpses surfaced.

What the US military had attempted to mask was that a flying saucer of extraterrestrial origin had crashed at Roswell, and they had hushed it up, preferring to study alien technology and biology in secret. The wreckage was brought to the ultra top-secret research base at Area 51 (see pages 122–123), where scientists were able to reverse-engineer new technologies, such as the Stealth Bomber, by working backward from super-advanced alien technology

to arrive at technology that humans could understand and use. Roswell marked the start of contact between the US authorities and space aliens. In the intervening years, there have been numerous retrievals of crashed Unidentified Flying Objects (UFOs) around the world.

The official line

The 1947 weather balloon story was indeed an example of disinformation. In 1997, the US Air Force released the document *Roswell: Case Closed*, which set out the story of what had happened: what crashed was a balloon from the top-secret Project Mogul, a program of high-altitude radar research.

The so-called "evidence of the UFO community" does not hold up to scrutiny. The "unearthly metals" were simply reflective material from the balloon. Tales of recovered bodies are garbled memories from 1950s balloon tests using crash-test dummies or possibly from the wreckage of a fuel plane where the corpses of the crew were badly burned. The nurse said to have passed on vital secret information never existed. The alien autopsy film is clearly an imposture: the "alien" an almost exact replica of a model used in a film about Roswell; the procedures bear no resemblance to a real autopsy.

The initial military release that started the clamor was simply the result of an over-eager local press officer with a head full of UFO talk (the mystery had begun just a few weeks earlier with the first reported sighting in Washington DC).

How paranoid should you be? 5%

The Roswell case initially offered some interesting glimpses into how the US military used disinformation as a device to hide top-secret research programs. It now seems likely that the authorities were happy to encourage public speculation about UFOs in the 1940s as a cover for the development of US research craft, such as the Skyhook balloons which were used to spy on Soviet nuclear tests. Sadly, the whole affair has now descended into tawdry farce with tacky UFO museums sprouting all over Roswell and no less than six "authentic crash sites" competing for tourist dollars.

Area 51

The US government is secretly building UFOs in collaboration with aliens to create human-alien hybrids for the purpose of world domination.

Area 51 is a secret research and testing ground based around the dry bed of Groom Lake in Nevada. The area was used for Army tests during the World War II but was then abandoned until 1955 when it was reopened for secret aviation testing. Area 51 borders the Nevada Test Site nuclear testing ground. It is variously known as Watertown, Dreamland, and Paradise Ranch.

What the theorists say

A series of local sightings involving strange lights and aerial phenomena indicate that something strange is going on in the area, while the incredibly tight safety measures of a private security force backed up by unmarked black helicopters show the extent to which the government is keen to hide something. It was suspected that the wreckage of the flying saucer that had crashed at Roswell, together with the bodies of its alien pilots (see pages 119–121), had been transferred to Area 51 to be tested and probed. This was confirmed by Bob Lazar, a former scientist at the base, who came forward during the 1980s to reveal the full story. Lazar maintained that US scientists had used the Roswell wreckage to reverse engineer their own advanced flying devices using an "exotic element," which had only recently been created by civilian scientists to provide power and anti-gravity. Lazar claims it was initially obtained through trade with an alien race. The research has taken place in a giant underground complex beneath Area 51.

The official line

The lurid theories about Area 51 are severely weakened by a total lack of evidence. Lazar's credibility is tenuous at best. Experts dispute his grasp of science, while he appears to have faked his academic record. There is no proof of underground levels at Area 51, which begs the question: what is the true role of this undoubtedly super-secret research facility? The US government neither confirms nor denies the existence of Area 51, but plenty is known about the history of the developments that took place there up until the early 1980s. The base was created for the CIA and its contractors, Lockheed Martin, to develop a range of advanced planes, starting with U2 spy aircraft, and followed by the SR71 Blackbird and F117 Stealth planes. Little is known about its activities since the 1980s, although there is much speculation. Some people claim that the base has now closed down and transferred operations to a new site in Utah.

How paranoid should you be? 27%

There is no evidence to link UFOs with Area 51 but the history and continued existence of the base *does* raise disturbing questions. Is it right for the CIA to be able to develop anything it likes, at a vast cost to the taxpayer, and without any oversight, particularly given that big business is profiting as a result? What kind of technology is being created and how is it being funded? Area 51 seems uncomfortably like a secret cash cow for the military-industrial complex.

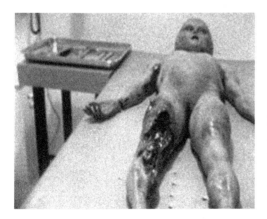

Left A photograph touted by Internet conspiracy theorists as documentary evidence of an autopsy of an alien carried out by the US government in top secret in Area 51.

The Rendlesham Incident

British and US authorities tried to cover up an extraordinary UFO encounter outside an American nuclear base in Britain.

In 1980, RAF Woodbridge was part of a two-base complex in Suffolk's Rendlesham Forest that was operated and occupied by the United States Air Force. Early in the morning of December 26, 1980, patrolmen were sent to investigate strange lights in the forest and two nights later Deputy Base Commander Lieutenant Colonel Charles Halt was called out again. British ufologists predictably went nuts—what seemed like the case of the century had landed on their doorstep. This "British Roswell" had everything: close encounters, physical evidence, credible eyewitnesses, actual recordings of events that confirmed their stories, and even corroboration from the highest level. Surely this was the case that would solve the UFO mystery once and for all.

What the theorists say

Halt submitted a report but neither the British or American authorities wanted to investigate further. This official intransigence began to look suspicious when ufologists began their own investigation and uncovered an incredible story. The three patrolmen on duty on the morning of the twenty-sixth reported encountering a glowing metallic triangular object in the woods, which moved off, leaving three holes in the shape of a triangle. Readings seemed to indicate high levels of radiation. Was this the elusive physical evidence that ufologists had been searching for?

One of the patrolmen later claimed to have touched the craft and sketched its strange markings. Halt reported seeing beams of light from UFOs apparently directed at the base's nuclear weapon bunkers, while a tape recording he made provided further proof of the encounter. His radio had stopped working and lights set up after the first incident mysteriously malfunctioned; radar traces of unidentified objects were recorded.

Meanwhile, a cover-up seemed to be in effect: a roll of film shot by one of the patrolmen never came back from the pharmacist and witnesses claimed to have been harassed by the authorities. A ufologist researching the case attempted to question Prime Minister Margaret Thatcher and her reply was "You can't tell the people!"

The official line

The real source of the strange lights seen in Rendlesham Forest was a nearby lighthouse. The initial reports made by the three patrolmen did not match their later testimonies. At the time, they claimed that they never got closer than 164 feet (50 meters) to the "object," and certainly never touched it. After chasing the lights through the woods, they realized that they had been looking at the nearby lighthouse all along.

There were also discrepancies in Halt's story. The timing and description reported on his tape showed that he, too, had almost certainly been looking at the lighthouse. His radio had never stopped working and there was nothing strange about the broken lights; they frequently malfunctioned. The "landing marks" supposedly made by the UFO were actually rabbit holes and the radiation readings proved to be normal for the area. The anomalous radar traces could have been due to either a meteor shower that occurred during this period or to the debris from a Russian satellite that was burning up in the atmosphere. There was no investigation because there simply was nothing to unearth. Margaret Thatcher's statement was misconstrued and simply meant that people refuse to listen to logical explanations of UFO sightings.

How paranoid should you be? 2%

The Rendlesham incident seems to have been comprehensively explained and most serious ufologists consider the case closed.

The Abduction Files

Thousands, perhaps millions, of people are regularly kidnapped by aliens and taken up on their spacecraft to be experimented on.

UFO sightings were common from 1947 onward but the first widely reported case of alien abduction was reported in 1957 when Barney and Betty Hill, both of whom suffered from nightmares and ill health after a sighting, visited a hypnotist for psychotherapy treatment. Under hypnosis, they described what has since become a familiar story: small aliens with green-gray skin and large, almond-shaped eyes had transported them on board a spacecraft for probing and medical tests before returning them to their car. When they regained consciousness several hours later, they had no memory of the events that had unfolded (a phenomenon known as "missing time").

The abduction phenomenon really took off in the 1980s after horror author Whitley Streiber published his bestseller, *Communion*, detailing his own abduction experiences. Meanwhile, Budd Hopkins, a New York artist, claimed to have gathered evidence that abductions were happening on a massive scale. Hundreds of people, under hypnosis or in group therapy, started to recall traumatic memories of alien abductions.

What the theorists say

The experiences reported by abductees tend to follow similar patterns, proof that they are describing something real. The abduction normally takes place from the person's bedroom or from a car being driven through a deserted place at night. Typically those who are abducted sense a strange presence while simultaneously losing control of their bodies. They are somehow transported into a spaceship, probed and experimented on, sometimes shown strange sights, then returned. These individuals have no recollection of the event in question but may notice memory gaps or "missing time." They may also suffer ill health, nightmares, and psychological problems.

Many claim that the aliens extract sperm or eggs or implant alien-human hybrid embryos. Some abductees claim to have detected and even recovered "implants," tiny devices of unknown origin or function lodged in their bodies, allegedly to help the aliens track them down.

There is evidence that abductions are shockingly common. According to one survey, 2 percent of Americans report experiences that indicate abduction; a total of 5 million people in America alone.

The official line

Almost all abduction memories appear through the suggestiveness of hypnotic therapy which has also been proven to give people "false" memories, convincing them of things that never happened. No physical proof of an abduction has yet been found—even implants mysteriously disappear before they can be investigated—while no one can explain how abductees move from their beds or cars into the waiting spaceships, often apparently passing through walls.

Many abduction-related experiences are symptomatic of non-paranormal conditions, such as sleep paralysis. This is a little-known but surprisingly common phenomenon where a sleeper's mind is working but their muscles remain paralyzed. Most muscles are immobile during REM (the dream phase of sleep) to prevent the individual from acting out their dreams and injuring themselves. Sufferers report sensations of fear, strange presences, and pressure on the chest. In earlier times, these experiences were often interpreted as attacks by supernatural beings, such as witches or demons, but in a modern context these creatures have been substituted for aliens. More prosaically, most abductions occur at night or when people are sleepy: might they simply be misremembered dreams?

How paranoid should you be? 0%

The uniformity of abduction experiences is evidence that they have a cultural rather than physical basis. Elements of this phenomenon, especially the appearance of the aliens, are well-known from popular culture. The Hill abduction, for instance, took place just after the broadcast of a television program featuring aliens with gray skin and big eyes. Perhaps the main message is that it *is* dangerous to be hypnotized by people with a harmful agenda because they can easily create false memories that may be deeply distressing.

Cattle Mutilation

Somebody or something is injuring or
killing cattle around the world with
surgical precision and the government
is trying to cover this up.

From the summer of 1973 until 1976, a wave of bovine mutilations
spread across the American Midwest. Genitals, eyes, and ears were gouged
out with surgical precision, flesh was stripped off the jaw, and blood was
drained from the bodies. No tracks or animal signs were ever found. In
Britain, there is a long history of "horse ripping": bizarre attacks on live
horses that continue to this day. Latin America is another mutilation
hotspot and the site of a related phenomenon where the presence of
mutilated, blood-drained livestock is blamed on a creature called the
chupacabras or "goatsucker."

What the theorists say

Many mutilation episodes are linked to UFO sightings, black helicopters, and
men in black, presumably government agents sent to harass witnesses. These
links are no coincidence. Cattle mutilations are the result of bizarre alien
experiments using biological material from Earth to create alien-earthling
hybrids and cyborgs. Earth governments are in league with them, providing
bases for their research labs (see Area 51, pages 122–123) and covering up for
them. The *chupacabras* is a bizarre hybrid created by alien-US scientists and
released into Latin America as an experiment. We know all this from
memories recovered from abductees and the testimony of insiders who have
worked within the conspiracy.

The official line

The mutilations have been extensively studied by the FBI and scientists, all
of whom have reached the same conclusion: the cattle were killed by normal

predators before their corpses were scavenged by other animals that only eat specific organs; the blood drained into the soil; and the "surgical precision" of the cuts was due to the sharp teeth of scavengers. For instance, the 1975 FBI report into the original mutilations explains, "State veterinarians, after examination of the mutilated animal carcasses, contend that dead animals were eaten by other animals or varmints, believed to be foxes due to their sharp side teeth, which were described as 'shearing teeth like scissors.'" There are no signs because scavengers are usually small animals and do not leave obvious tracks. In Latin America, a tiny mouse species is blamed for some mutilations; the case for this was strengthened when such rodents were caught gnawing off the noses and ears of cattle.

Accounts by conspiracy theorists are unsupported by the evidence. Recovered memories are not reliable; "insiders" are frauds. The theories make no sense. Why would aliens collect body parts from privately owned cattle? How would this genetic material be of use to aliens? The pseudo-scientific conspiracy theories reveal a shocking ignorance of basic biology.

How paranoid should you be? 2%

These "waves" follow a similar pattern. Media reports of a few cases spread panic, leading to more reported cases. The authorities dispatch the experts and investigations are undertaken. They confirm that there is no paranormal agency; dogs, coyotes, and other predators or scavengers are to blame. With the mystery "solved," media interest dies away but farmers who experience extensive cattle loss to predators remain convinced that something supernatural is at work.

The Dark Side Hypothesis

All strands of the US-government UFO cover-up come together in a conspiracy to take over the world and bring about the Apocalypse.

By 1980, ufology was riddled with sinister reports of "Grays," visitors with slanted eyes and undefined features, who traveled in triangular spacecraft, mutilated cattle, abducted humans, and were seemingly protected by government helicopters and agents. How were these elements linked?

Paul Bennewitz was investigating strange lights near an Air Force base when he began to receive classified information from inside the military. Thanks to his writings, the truth about the Dark Side was revealed to an incredulous world.

What the theorists say

The Dark Side hypothesis maintains that a secret world government is in league with an alien race. The conspiracy began in 1947 with the retrieval of a crashed space saucer at Roswell, after which President Truman set up a secret council called MJ-12 (MJ stands for "Majestic" or "Majority") to deal with the issue of UFOs. Leaked government documents sensationally confirm the existence of this organization.

Further retrievals of spacecraft wreckage and live and dead alien specimens were concealed from the public until the 1954 meeting at Holloman Air Force Base between the US government and a race of aliens known as "Grays," just one of several alien races frequently visiting planet Earth. The "Grays" needed genetic terrestrial material to revive their dwindling race and the government agreed to co-operate in return for advanced technology. Secret bases, such as Area 51, were allocated to the aliens and covert forces helped to implement a program of cattle mutilation and abductions.

MJ-12 operated as a secret government-within-a-government using mind-control technology, implants, and engineered diseases to control population numbers and prepare the human race for colonization. It established bases on Mars and the "dark side" of the Moon. To fund its activities, the secret government, through its control of the world's intelligence and security apparatus, started trading in drugs and assassinations. Eventually a New World Order will be proclaimed where alien-human hybrids will rule the Earth and humans will become slaves. For paranoiacs of a religious bent, the Dark Side conspiracy is a preparation for the Apocalypse.

The official line

The only pieces of evidence for this theory are the leaked MJ-12 documents and the "inside" testimony fed to Bennewitz. The FBI launched a probe and concluded that the documents were bogus. The testimony has since been revealed to be disinformation originating with Richard Doty, an officer from the Air Force Office of Special Investigations responsible for looking into UFO reports. Doty worked in league with ufologist William Moore to feed disinformation to the mentally unstable Bennewitz, who eventually had a breakdown. Moore has since admitted his role in the deception while Doty was discharged from the Air Force.

How paranoid should you be? 0%

The hypothesis is clearly paranoid nonsense but the role of Doty raises intriguing questions. Why did the government go to so much effort to create the Dark Side movement? Ufologists now believe that the authorities have been engaged in a 50-year disinformation campaign as cover for top-secret activities, such as nuclear weapons retrieval, advanced flight projects, and surveillance missions.

The Aurora Research Project

At a facility in the Arctic, the US
government is conducting top-secret
experiments in weather modification,
beam weapons, and mind control.

The High Frequency Active Auroral Research Program (known as HAARP) is
an array of high-power radio transmitters at a research station in Alaska. It
was constructed by the Air Force Research Laboratory and Office of Naval
Research but is officially operated as an independent research station.
HAARP transmits high-frequency (HF) radio signals into the ionosphere (an
electrically charged layer of the upper atmosphere) to cause slight heating.
This changes its electrical properties, which can generate extremely low-
frequency (ELF) radio waves. Unlike normal radio waves, ELF waves can
penetrate almost anything and travel through ice, water, and rock.

What the theorists say

HAARP and its ionospheric heating effect are used for various nefarious
purposes. The heated region can be made to fire a beam of charged particles

Left Antennae at the HAARP
research station in Alaska. Are
these simply research apparatus
for physicists, or are they tools
used for a more sinister
purpose, such as controlling
weather patterns of enemy
nations or even controlling
human minds?

that are able to shoot down missiles as part of the Star Wars missile defense scheme, and even planes or spacecraft. HAARP tests were responsible for bringing down TWA 800 (see pages 74–76) and destroying the space shuttle *Columbia* in 2003. HAARP can also be used to modify the weather, inflicting droughts, storms, floods, and even hurricanes, on enemy nations. Because ELF radio waves operate at the same frequency as the electrical activity of the human brain, the ELF signals generated by HAARP are used as a sophisticated mind-control device, beaming out messages, thoughts, and instructions to the world's population.

The official line

HAARP is mainly used to study the physics of the ionosphere and Earth's electrical field, particularly the effects of solar wind. The ELF radio effect could be helpful for communicating with submerged submarines and for ground-penetrating radar to find bunkers, for instance, but research into this is probably in its infancy. There is no way for the HF beam to affect the troposphere or stratosphere—the atmospheric layers where weather happens—and the ionosphere does not influence the weather. The effects of HAARP in the ionosphere are negligible compared to the effects of solar activity, such as sun storms, which do affect day-to-day weather. As for biological effects, according to the HAARP website, the ELF signal generated by the ionospheric heating is "one million times weaker (smaller) than the level where researchers have reported biological effects in the literature."

How paranoid should you be? 10%

For a supposedly covert research and weapons facility, HAARP is not very secret. There is plenty of information about it on the public record and it even holds open days each year for the curious. Although some of the research with possible military applications remains classified, the scientific community as a whole seems convinced that the effects produced by HAARP are negligible compared to those that are naturally occurring. Where the complexity of science leaves a vacuum of ignorance and misunderstanding, conspiracy theories will rush in to fill the void.

MK-ULTRA and the Real Manchurian Candidates

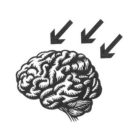

Was a thriller released in 1962 featuring a brainwashed assassin really fiction, or were the CIA and Army attempting mind control?

The 1960s thriller *The Manchurian Candidate* (a film remade in 2004) features the story of a brainwashed assassin. There is disturbing evidence that the CIA was indeed involved in an attempt at mass mind control.

Congressional and Army investigations during the 1970s revealed that in 1953 the CIA instigated a secret project called MK-ULTRA. Frightened by reports that during the Korean War communists had used brainwashing techniques to convert captured US soldiers, the CIA decided to develop its own mind-control methods. Under MK-ULTRA, drugs, radiation, and other techniques were tested on subjects, mostly without their knowledge.

The project included many shocking abuses. Mental patients were given LSD on a daily basis and subjected to psychological torture, fed intravenous cocktails of barbiturates and amphetamines, or put into comas for months and then played looped voice recordings. Many were irreparably damaged and at least two were killed. A CIA officer called Frank Olson, for example, was given LSD and fell to his death, supposedly during a psychotic episode. Twenty years of research eventually convinced the authorities that such techniques were not reliable or effective. From 1976, a series of presidential decrees made it illegal to carry out research without informed consent.

What the theorists say

Contrary to the official line, MK-ULTRA research was successful, a fact hard to prove given that then Director Richard Helms illegally ordered most of the files to be destroyed in 1972. Olson's death was not drug-induced suicide but murder. He had been part of a team sent to Europe to interrogate Cold War prisoners and was going to speak out. When his body was exhumed, it was shown that he had been knocked unconscious before falling to his death.

The methods developed by the program (active to this day) include ELF radio wave technology (see The Aurora Research Project, pages 133–134), drug control, hypnosis, and subliminal messaging. They were used during the siege of the Branch Dravidian compound at Waco, on the illegal detainees at Guatanamo Bay, on prisoners at Abu Ghraib prison, and in the War on Terror. Sections of the population are routinely controlled in this way; many schizophrenics are misdiagnosed victims of mind control techniques gone wrong.

The official line

The program was an outrageous abuse of power but it showed that such techniques do not work. Modern conspiracy claims are contradicted by how little we know about brain processes. How *does* the brain create thoughts, emotions, or consciousness? Scare stories about communist hypnotic brainwashing proved to be false. Presidential decrees mean that this sort of thing no longer goes on and there is no evidence to suggest that anything other than "stressing" techniques were employed in the War on Terror.

How paranoid should you be? 66%

The mind control hypothesized by paranoiacs is pure science fiction but the shocking abuses of MK-ULTRA may well be real. The US ignored international conventions on torture and used similar techniques at Guantanamo and Abu Ghraib, and its intelligence services are operating a private airline to ferry prisoners to despotic regimes in order to circumvent US rules and oversight. Given the track record of these agencies, it is *extremely* plausible that prisoners are being interrogated using the dangerous drug or psychological techniques derived from the program.

Psychic Spying

The CIA and the US Department of Defense spent millions of dollars on developing a 20-year psychic espionage program.

Like the MK-ULTRA program (see pages 135–136), America's psychic spying equivalent, known as Operation Stargate, had its genesis in Cold War paranoia about what the "other side" was up to, with reports leaking out of the Soviet Union that the Communist "Reds" were seriously researching psychic powers. The CIA, not wanting to fall behind, commissioned Harold Puthoff and Russell Targ of the Stanford Research Institute to investigate a form of extrasensory perception (ESP) known as remote viewing (RV), or astral travel, in which a psychic mentally journeys to a distant location to watch and listen, passing through walls if necessary. The results they achieved convinced the Department of Defense (DoD) to take over the project and establish it as Operation Stargate.

Together with the National Security Agency, the DoD spent some $20 million over the next 20 years, recruiting psychics and training them in these clairvoyant techniques. In 1995, the CIA commissioned an outside audit which concluded that Operation Stargate had no value and was a waste of public money. The program was duly shut down leaving the "psychic spies" to fend for themselves. Several became public speakers and lecturers on RV.

What the theorists say

According to the ex-psychic spies, they were incredibly successful, helping the Army and the National Security Agency (NSA) to locate kidnapped generals, Palestine Liberation Organization (PLO) training camps, crashed aircraft, and secret Soviet submarine bases. If remote viewing failed to work, why did the DoD continue to fund the operation for so long? It only ran into trouble when the original military psychic spies were supplemented by new recruits from civilian, New Age, and occult backgrounds. Some RV practitioners claim still to be working with or for the security services today, helping to track down terrorists and prevent attacks.

The official line

The extended lifespan of the program is simply a testament to the poor critical thinking skills and scientific training of the officers in charge. Psychologists have identified a range of non-paranormal tactics used by so-called "psychics," such as making very long, rambling statements to increase their chances of success, and being vague, which starts to explain why RV seemed to work. Operation Stargate was run as an intelligence operation, not an experiment, so the psychic spies were given as much information about the "targets" as possible, such as satellite photos and descriptions. No wonder they appeared to make some very accurate guesses. The 1995 review concluded that even if the psychics were genuine, intelligence obtained in this fashion was worthless since it had to be first verified by conventional means.

How paranoid should you be? 0%

It seems certain that the CIA, NSA, and DoD effectively fell for the same tricks that showbiz psychics use on stage. But this was not simply harmless fun. An essential part of RV training was in techniques that boosted mental imagery and imagination; these practices weakened the psychic spies' grasp on reality and encouraged fantasizing and delusions. Some of them were mentally scarred for life.

Sources

Internet

Wikipedia: *www.wikipedia.org*
Disinfopedia: *www.disinfopedia.org*
Lobster: *www.lobster-magazine.co.uk/intro/index.php*
Counterpunch: *www.counterpunch.org*
Parascope: *www.parascope.com*
The Konformist: *www.konformist.com*
Paranoia: The Conspiracy Reader: *www.paranoiamagazine.com*
Conspiracy Planet—the Alternative News and History Network: *www.conspiracyplanet.com*
Illuminati Conspiracy Archive: *www.conspiracyarchive.com*
Quackwatch: *www.quackwatch.org*

Literature

Ahmed, Kamal, "Britain framed Irish hero with 'jubilee plot' to murder Victoria" (*The Observer* May 12, 2002)

Bryson, Chris, "The Donora Fluoride Fog" (*Earth Island Journal*: 1998)

Carroll, Robert Todd, *The Skeptic's Dictionary* (John Wiley & Sons: Hoboken, 2003)

Counterpunch magazine (PO Box 228, Petrolia, CA 95558)

Dash, Mike, *Borderlands* (Arrow Books: London, 1998)

Fortean Times (Box 2409, London NW5 4NP; *www.forteantimes.com*)

Jay, Mike, *Emperors of Dreams* (Dedalus: Sawtry, 2000)

Lean, Michael and Hankey, Catherine, "Aspartame and its effects on health" (*British Medical Journal*: 2004)

Levy, Joel, *The KISS Guide to the Unexplained* (Dorling Kindersley: London, 2002)

Levy, Joel, *Secret History: Hidden forces that shaped the past* (Vision: London, 2004)

Lobster: The Journal of Parapolitics (Robin Ramsay (Dept. W), 214 Westbourne Avenue, Hull HU5 3JB, United Kingdom)

Miller, T Christian, "Post-invasion chaos blamed for drugs surge" (*LA Times*, October 4, 2004)

Ramsay, Robin, *Conspiracy Theories* (Pocket Essentials: Harpenden, 2000)

Rickard, Bob and Michell John, *The Rough Guide to Unexplained Phenomena* (Rough Guides: London, 2000)

Ronson, Jon, *Them: Adventures with Extremists* (Picador: London, 2001)

Vankin, Jonathan and Whalen, John, *The 80 Greatest Conspiracies of All Time* (Citadel Press: New York, 2004)

Glossary

beam weapons: firearms that emit energy beams.

Biblical Reconstructionist: individuals who believe in the Bible's literal truth and the need to actively prepare the world for the Second Coming.

Bilderberg: a private think-tank/discussion group founded in 1954 to further dialog between opinion makers and policy formers in Europe and North America.

bioterror: terrorism carried out with biological weapons such as anthrax.

black budget: funds allocated without oversight, possibly illegally.

black helicopters: unmarked aircraft used by secret agencies for covert operations.

black ops: illegal covert operations.

brainwashed: caused to believe or act in ways contrary to normal behavior; some form of mind control.

chemtrail: chemical residue left by a plane through spraying or as part of the exhaust.

Central Intelligence Agency (CIA): US foreign intelligence agency set up in 1945 as the successor to the Office of Strategic Services (OSS).

conspiracy: secret plan by two or more people to do something illegal or immoral.

Contras: from the Spanish *contrarevolucionario* ("counterrevolutionary"); right-wing paramilitaries opposed to the post-1979 Sandinista Nicaraguan government.

Council on Foreign Relations: private US think-tank/discussion group concerned with improving US foreign policy and relations and developing foreign policy talent.

covert ops: secret or undercover operations.

cover-up: attempt to obscure the truth.

cyborgs: machine–animal hybrids.

Drug Enforcement Administration (DEA): US agency concerned with domestic and foreign drug trafficking.

disinformation: deliberately misleading information.

false memory: bogus recollections created by hypnosis or other forms of therapy, believed to be genuine by the individual concerned.

Federal Bureau of Investigation (FBI): US law enforcement agency concerned with domestic counter-espionage and counter-terrorism, among other functions.

free energy: energy from abundant, easily accessible sources that costs nothing or next-to-nothing to produce.

fundamentalist: anyone with extreme beliefs who refuses to accept the legitimacy of alternative beliefs.

Illuminati: in conspiracy circles, an arch-conspiracy group believed to be manipulating world history.

insurgency: rebellion or revolution.

lone gunman: assassin or shooter who acts on his own; the opposite of a conspiracy.

Manchurian candidate: brainwashed assassin activated by post-hypnotic suggestion.

men in black (MIB): mysterious government agents of unspecified origin associated with strange phenomena and engaged in cover-ups.

MI5: the Security Service; British domestic intelligence agency.

MI6: the Secret Intelligence Service; British foreign intelligence agency.

military-industrial complex: associated military and business interests, such as suppliers and weapons manufacturers; together they form a powerful bloc of interests.

military-security complex: range of military, intelligence and law-enforcement agencies, and their associated bureaucracies and stakeholders.

militia: military force raised from the civilian population; in US, often refers to armed right-wing survivalists and/or anti-governmental groups.

mind control: causing someone to think or behave without their conscious assent or awareness.

money laundering: handling illegally obtained ("dirty") money so it appears to have come from a legitimate source.

narco-state: country that depends mainly on the production and trafficking of illegal narcotics to support its economy.

Neoconservatives (Neocons): radical right-wing ideologs who believe in American interventionism.

new world order: in conspiracy circles, the aim of a global conspiracy, involving the suppression of democracy and the enslavement of all world peoples under a single global dictatorship. In political terms, a major rebalancing of global power.

National Security Agency (NSA): US agency responsible for eavesdropping on communications of all types.

oversight: in politics, the process of monitoring or reviewing the actions and accounts of an agency or body to ensure it remains democratically accountable.

P2: a secret Masonic group with connections to organized crime, right-wing politics, and the Catholic Church, especially in Italy and Latin America.

paramilitaries: armed groups not belonging to an official state military or law enforcement agency.

parapolitics: politics carried out through underhand means.

Pentagon: home to the Department of Defense (DoD); shorthand reference to it.

pseudoscience: system of thought and practice that falsely claims to be scientific and uses the trappings of science to lend authority to itself.

psy-ops: psychological operations with a psychological effect, such as demoralizing or disorienting an enemy.

radionics: (pseudo)science of electromagnetic vibrations in living things.

recovered memory: recollections only accessible through post-hypnosis or other forms of therapy.

remote viewing (RV): psychic ability to mentally travel to a distant location to watch and listen.

reverse engineering: process of working backward from super-advanced alien technology to technology humans can understand and use.

saucer retrieval: recovery of crashed alien spacecraft for study and concealment.

secret services: government agencies concerned with intelligence-gathering and covert operations.

security services: government agencies concerned with maintaining order and/or using force; umbrella term for military, police, and intelligence agencies.

sleep paralysis: phenomenon where a sleeper's mind rises out of sleep into consciousness but the muscles remain paralyzed. Sufferers report sensations of fear, strange presences, and pressure on the chest.

State Department: department of the US government that deals with foreign affairs.

The Agency: see CIA.

Trilateral Commission: private think-tank/discussion group founded in 1973 to promote cooperation between Japan, North America, and Europe.

Unidentified Flying Object (UFO): technically any unexplained aerial phenomenon but usually used to mean an alien spacecraft.

ufology: study of UFOs and related issues carried out by ufologists.

War on Terror: post-9/11 effort to crack down on terrorist groups around the world.

weapons of mass destruction: nuclear, chemical, or biological weaponry capable of causing large-scale death and destruction.

Index

Page numbers in *italics* refer to illustrations